Ghostly Tales of Iowa

Ruth D. Hein *and* Vicky L. Hinsenbrock

Adventure Publications, Inc.
Cambridge, Minnesota

Dedication from Ruth:
To my father, Reverend William Ullerich, and my mother, Emma Ullerich (who would be surprised that I wrote these stories), and my native state of Iowa.

Dedication from Vicky:
To my parents, Dick and Bev Hinsenbrock.
To my nieces, Kelly, Kara and Stacy and their mother, my sister, Kim.
To my great niece, Brooke.
To my husband, Charlie, who puts up with my clutter and my books and loves me all the same.
And to David W., Carl B., and Alan K., who all left this world much too soon.

Thanks to all who responded to our request for ghost stories from Iowa. The time you took to tell us about your experiences and to answer our questions made the book possible. Thanks also to friends and relatives for helping us find stories.

With generous help from librarians and historical society personnel, we researched settings and backgrounds for the stories in documents, newspapers and other publications. In some cases, names and locations are disguised to respect the wishes of the storygivers.

Book and cover design by Jonathan Norberg

First Edition published by Iowa State University Press in Ames, Iowa, in 1996.

Second Edition
Copyright 2005 by Ruth D. Hein and Vicky L. Hinsenbrock
Published by:
Adventure Publications, Inc.
820 Cleveland Street South
Cambridge, MN 55008
1-800-678-7006
www.adventurepublications.net
ISBN-10: 1-59193-127-4
ISBN-13: 978-1-59193-127-0
All rights reserved
Printed in the U.S.A.

Table of Contents

Preface

The stories in this book came from different people and places in Iowa. Many are from northeast Iowa because some of them were published in our earlier book, *Ghostly Tales of Northeast Iowa* (1988).

Iowans were willing and, in fact, eager to share their stories with us, so that we could share them with our readers. Some of the stories are well known—for example, those connected with the house outside Guttenberg, or Lawther Hall and the Strayer-Wood Theater on the UNI campus in Cedar Falls. But others are stories that have been handed down through generations from grandparents and great-grandparents. And some happened in the last few years.

We hope you enjoy these new and old Iowa ghost stories. Some will give you chills; some will make you laugh. But all have a place in Iowa's history of storytelling.

Back to Her Grave

It was about dusk on a crisp but cloudy fall night about 1900. A young man we'll call Tom started home from Dorchester in his single-seat buggy. His faithful though somewhat jumpy stallion, appropriately named Spook, would take him the twelve or thirteen miles or so toward Waukon to where Tom lived on a small farm.

While crossing a dry run, the tugs on the harness slackened a little and one came unhooked. Tom, quite agile at age twenty, quickly leaped down from the buggy without stopping and fastened the tug again. Then, with one hand on the side bar of the seat, he heaved himself back up into the buggy.

Much to his surprise and not much to his liking, there sat a lady passenger beside him. She was dressed in black and wore a black broad-brimmed hat with a black veil hiding her face. That was all he could see, even at close range, since there was no moonlight to help him out.

Tom had no idea who she was or how she got there so quickly. All he knew was that he wanted to get home as fast as possible. Tom knew that Spook couldn't have seen her approach the buggy, because he would have reacted to this strange figure if he had seen her. But when Tom slapped the reins, Spook bolted into a frenzied gallop. Though horse and buggy were nearly out of control, Spook miraculously managed to stay on the curvy road.

No one else was out on that stretch of road at the time. The strange passenger didn't say a word, and Tom was too dumfounded to start up a conversation with her. He wished Spook would slow down so he himself could tumble out and leave the ghost or whatever it was to tear off into the darkness with the galloping horse. But Spook knew the road well and kept going at that wild speed for several miles.

Soon Tom was aware that he and his uninvited passenger were approaching the country church called Hanover and the cemetery near it. The cemetery had been in use since 1889—just about a year.

Alongside the burial ground, the darkly dressed passenger somehow leaped or floated from the buggy. Tom could just manage to see her shape as she ran as fast as the stallion. But Spook stayed on the road, and the woman ran into the cemetery and disappeared into an open grave just as Spook rounded the next curve and left the cemetery behind.

Ray Burke of Waukon told this story. His father told it to him when Ray was about six. Ray's father, born in 1890, was only about ten when the incident happened, but he heard the story many times from his father, who enjoyed telling it every chance he had.

In the 1950s, the old road was paved and became Highway 13. Now it's State Highway 76. The dry run is still there, overlapped with a culvert. When Ray was a boy, there was a small, narrow cement bridge over it and Ray admits that as a small boy he was terrified of even going by the dry run and the bridge. By then, he was riding in the family's old Model A Ford, but he sincerely hoped they wouldn't have a flat tire right about there.

Even if Hanover hasn't been put on a road map of Iowa since about 1960, the dry run is still there, and Dorchester and Waukon are on the map. And if you looked for it you could probably find the Hanover cemetery, too. But I leave it to your discretion whether to look for that particular grave.

Barney's Still Around

It was opening night at The Landmark. Everything was in order. Dick and Diane had worked hard to ready their supper club for this night. After the remodeling was completed, finishing touches were added: old photos, an old-fashioned wall telephone, an antique buffet, "railroad chairs" and other items reminiscent of the early years when the building had been known as The Landmark Inn.

When they heard car doors closing and people coming in the front door, Dick and Diane went downstairs to welcome their guests. Dick stopped off at the kitchen first to check whether the cooks were ready. Diane took one last look around the dining area before she went to greet a group of customers off to one side of the room. After several well-deserved compliments on how inviting the atmosphere was, someone asked her, "Has anything happened yet?"

Diane's first impulse was to answer, "Well, yes! We've changed the building a lot, put gobs of money and work into it—can't you see the difference?" when a loud noise made it unnecessary for her to answer at all. The noise came from upstairs, where Dick and Diane's living quarters were. It sounded as though something quite heavy had fallen to the floor up there. A couple of customers' smiles faded.

Diane excused herself to go back upstairs. As she went up, she thought, No one is supposed to be up here! What she found was the large photo of her parents not on the bedside table, but on the floor. Mostly it was intact; and just a small corner of the glass was chipped.

But she knew that the photo had been placed so that it could not fall off by itself. Realizing its cast iron frame made it so heavy that it made the loud noise, she put it back and went downstairs.

As she rejoined the group, one woman asked a bit hesitantly, "Um...was it Barney?"

This group of customers and others who had lived in the area for a long time knew the history of the building. They had read about it in *The History of Allamakee County* and in the book *Past and Present of Allamakee County*. They knew that the main house was built in 1851 as a private residence by Colonel John A. Wakefield. At a very young age he had been a scout in the war of 1812–1815. Wakefield then studied medicine and law and was admitted to the bar in 1818. He enlisted in the army and fought in The Blackhawk Indian War. Afterward, he served as a judge in St. Paul before moving to Allamakee County in northeast Iowa. He apparently was given the land on Lansing Ridge in 1851, and on it he built the grand, two-story house.

Under changing ownership the building had later housed a brewery, a hotel and residence, a tearoom and restaurant, and a general store, post office, bar, gas station and dance hall before it had become and remained a restaurant.

They knew about the waitress who had seen Barney during a previous ownership. The knew he had been around for a long time.

Many years ago, when an old stage road went by there, the stagecoach stop was up the road about a mile, near the three-story, hand-built, rock school named the Lycurgus School. Back in the days when passengers and the mail and other important cargo went by stagecoach to various destinations, passengers often stayed at the Landmark Inn for the night.

When one of the succession of owners operated a brewery in the building, drivers and teamsters found it an ideal place to visit while their horses rested. The men often spent the evening enjoying food and drink before their next run. Sometimes the natural competitiveness already present among them, augmented by a few drinks, led to arguments as to who was the better driver—or the faster driver—or who had the fastest horses or the smoothest-riding rig.

Late one night, when most of the weary travelers had slaked their thirst and had retired to their rooms upstairs at the inn, the arguments developed into a fight on the lower level. The result was that a teamster named Barney Leavy was killed. That's about all anyone knows about it now, except that later owners claim that Barney's ghost still haunts the place.

Diane recalled the many questions asked of them while they worked at the remodeling. She knew that the story about Barney had been perpetuated over the years. She could add to the story, if she felt so inclined. She could tell about the strange noises and flickering lights in the old building, when they first came to it. A light in the kitchen often came back on after they had turned it off. And she remembered something that happened just once when they were first remodeling the building. It was in the middle of winter. They were working in the main dining room. When they locked up at night, everything was okay. But when they came back the next morning, there was a big pool of water on the floor in the middle of the room. She said, "There's a second floor, so it wasn't a leaky roof. And there was snow on the ground at the time, but we didn't find any tracks outside. And we checked the locks. They were all right. At the time, Dick looked at me sort of funny and he said, 'Barney?'"

So Barney must still be around. If you want to meet him, you'll find the former inn, now called The Landmark, on State Highway 9 between Waukon and Lansing about a mile and a half from Churchtown in northeast Iowa. Dick and Diane Prestemon operate it as a supper club—one with a past.

A Bootlegger's Ghost?

Evelyn enjoyed working in her kitchen. She said it was the most pleasant room in the old house in Clinton. Sometime in the summer of 1966, she and Paul and their six daughters had moved into that house. It had been built around the turn of the century.

Clinton is on the eastern border of Iowa, and the house was only two blocks from the Mississippi River. The basement had been flooded during the 1965 flood. Evelyn said, "That's why we never used it. I never even went down there. It stank of the river water."

The arrangement of the rooms made the house a bit unhandy. Evelyn called it "an odd arrangement," but she knew it was only temporary housing. She said the house had two bedrooms and a bath upstairs, two bedrooms down, and a half bath-laundry off the kitchen. There was a tiny entry, but it was necessary to go through the living room to get anywhere else in the house. The stairway to the upstairs was behind a door in that same living room. The steps were uncarpeted, so anyone going up or down could, in ordinary circumstances, be easily heard.

Evelyn and Paul used the downstairs bedroom that faced the front of the house; the entry was to one side of it. As Evelyn said, "It wasn't very much like the houses we had been used to, but we could make it work out, for a while."

Evelyn developed what she called a bad habit while they lived there. Maybe it was because the roomy and well-arranged kitchen with its soft yellow walls and its windows on each side was so pleasant. She got to doing the dishes late, after the rest of the family had gone to bed.

Sometimes, down there in the kitchen, she heard footsteps behind her. She just thought someone couldn't sleep, but when she turned around, there was never anyone else in the room. It happened more than once, so one night Evelyn did something about it. She verbally confronted the unseen presence. She said, "I wish you would either speak, or go about your business! I have plenty to do here." Then she heard footsteps going down to the cellar. Of course, she didn't follow, since the cellar was unpleasant enough to keep her out of it as it was.

The same thing happened often enough that Evelyn changed her habit. She started hurrying to get the dishes done early. Somehow, that put an end to the footsteps behind her in the kitchen. Maybe her unseen visitor didn't like calling at an earlier hour.

Later that year, though, Evelyn heard the footsteps again. This time they were louder and they seemed to be out on the wooden porch, at night. Evelyn tried to wake Paul, but he did not wake up.

The sound of heavy footsteps on the porch happened several times. Then came the Christmas season. The family put up their tall, live tree a day or so before Christmas, as usual. They liked to keep their decorated trees up until Twelfth Night, January sixth. On the day after New Year's, Evelyn woke up smelling the odor of a burning house. She looked around, and she checked the tree, but she could find nothing to account for the odor. That experience was just scary enough to make her decide to take the tree down earlier than Twelfth Night. That same day, she dismantled it. Right away, the smell of something burning went away.

That Christmas, a gift to each daughter was a complete set of bed linens. Every pattern and color was different. Eventually, the girls made their beds up with the new sheets and pillowcases and enjoyed their smell of "newness." But the first time Ruth used her new sheets, something happened that frightened the girls. That night, Mary and Judith (the two oldest girls) raced downstairs and tried to wake their father. Their mother woke up instead. The girls hurried her upstairs to see their sister Ruth's sheet. Evelyn said, "It had some strange slashes on the side. They were about an inch long and they looked like claw marks.

"That was when I learned that I wasn't the only one in the family that had been having strange encounters. Up until then, I hadn't told anyone. But when the girls told me they'd been hearing footsteps coming up the uncarpeted steps and to the door of their room, I told them about my unexplainable experiences, too.

"The girls said that when they first heard the steps, they thought it was one of us coming upstairs and toward their door; but they said the footsteps sounded heavier than we did when we came up."

The older girls told their mother that the same thing had happened three or four times. Then Judith said, "Tonight, the door seemed to open but was really still shut, and the footsteps went over toward the window where Ruth was sleeping. She didn't wake up, even when Mary and I tried to wake her. The others in the front bedroom went right on sleeping, too, while we looked in shock at those claw marks on Ruth's sheet."

Evelyn said, "We didn't know what to make of all this. Then, before long—it was around Ash Wednesday—we read a death notice for an elderly woman who had once lived in that house. She was over ninety when she died. After her funeral, we never heard anything else unusual in our house—no unfamiliar footsteps, for sure. When someone told us that the deceased woman's husband had been a bootlegger during the twenties and had died by violence, we wondered if it was his ghost that was hanging around. Did he come back to wait for his wife? Or did he come back to check the basement, to see if the flood waters had ruined his operation or had revealed his secrets? Was the cellar his 'haunt,' or was it the place where he entered the house and left again?"

Evelyn said, "We moved out in March of that same year. The house is gone now. But in a church group, I met a woman who had lived there before we did. She said she had had similar experiences with the footsteps and had smelled the burning odor at Christmas, but her husband didn't let her tell me about it and I never got to talk with her again. It seems that neither her husband nor mine ever noticed anything unusual there, and I could not find any record of a fire on that property.

"Whenever I asked others about the house, I found that most people who had any knowledge were very reluctant to talk about it."

Casper's Closet

Doug and Linda Hill lived in Grinnell, Iowa, in a white two-story four-bedroom home in a new addition at the edge of town. There were no large trees around it to "scritch against the windows, nothing to make it spooky," Linda said. They were the first occupants.

They had just returned home from the funeral of a relative in Clarion. It was in the fall of 1977. They had a two-year-old daughter named Erin, and they were expecting their second child in November.

Once home, and Erin was tucked in, Doug and Linda realized how tired they were, so they also went to bed and were sleeping soundly when they both heard three loud knocks—not at the outside doors, but on their bedroom wall. Both of them sat up in bed quickly and simultaneously asked, "What was that?"

Between their room and the nursery, all ready for the new baby's arrival, was a closet. It was just an ordinary closet, where they kept their clothing. When they realized the knocks had come from inside the closet, they got out of bed to check it, but could find nothing unusual. No clothing was out of place. Everything seemed to be in order, so they went back to bed and forgot about the incident.

They forgot about it, until they were awakened out of sound sleep—more than once—over the course of the next several weeks. Each time, they heard three loud knocks coming from the closet. When they told friends about it, they were told it was probably just the weather or the heating system or the plumbing. They said, "You know how the walls can crack when the temps change." Or they said, "We've had that happen. It's in the heating system or the plumbing." But Linda said, "We knew it wasn't."

They drew the conclusion that a ghost had come to stay with them and was making its presence known with the loud knocking. Linda said, "We called him Casper, the only name we could think of for a friendly ghost. And though we didn't appreciate being awakened in the middle of the night, Casper was never naughty or mischievous, so we were never really afraid. We just accepted him and went about our business."

One night shortly before their son Ryan was born, Linda was having trouble sleeping. She said, "I went downstairs to read a while so Doug could get a sound night's sleep. From all the way downstairs, I heard three loud knocks again. I knew it had to be Casper and that he wanted me to hear his knocks. It was as if he was getting serious, although about what, I'm sure I don't know. Doug came running down to see if I'd heard the noise, too.

"About a week later, Ryan made his entrance into our lives and we brought home the fourth member of our family. For a while then, with a new baby and a two-year-old to take care of, we were too busy to worry about ghosts.

"Ryan's nursery was right next to our bedroom, and what we dubbed 'Casper's closet' was between the two. As most babies do, Ryan often awoke in the night and cried for attention. A couple of months later, we realized that we hadn't heard Casper for quite a while. All we could figure out was that he got tired of listening to the crying baby and decided to go somewhere less noisy to 'live.'

"We haven't experienced anything else that we couldn't explain in some rational way since then. So although we haven't had a ghost since that time, we still think fondly on Casper's brief stay with us. In fact, we sort of miss him. We find ourselves wondering sometimes where he is, and who he is haunting now, and whether he'll ever come back to 'his closet' to 'live,' no matter who else occupies the house.

"We left the house in Grinnell and moved to Cedar Rapids when Ryan was in second grade. Later, we moved to Decorah. Casper apparently didn't follow us. All the knocks we've heard since then have been either at the front or the back door, and they were made by someone human that we didn't have to make up a name for."

And, since they were the first occupants of the house Casper also frequented for a while in Grinnell, they wonder how the house could have had a ghost. If anyone had died a sudden or violent death there, which is sometimes given as a reason for the presence of a ghost, it must have been on the land there. Or maybe there had once been a claim shanty or a log cabin or even a sod dugout on that spot in the days of early settlement. But they themselves had seen no evidence of an earlier home there. And if the builders or other new occupants in that new addition had, Doug and Linda didn't hear about it. As Linda said, "We just accepted Casper. We were too busy with our young family to worry about him."

The Cellar Witch

Clayton County in northeast Iowa was settled largely by German immigrants. Most of these were thrifty, hard working, sensible farmers from the "old country." But even these practical folk had ghostly stories.

A young lady and her parents had come to America when she was a small child. As she grew older, Clara wanted to be out on her own more. Clara's mother had warned her several times not to dawdle on her way to and from town. Her mother especially warned Clara and her sisters to stay away from a certain house in town, vacant now but rumored to have been lived in by a witch. Many people believed the witch's spirit still resided in the house.

Clara knew she shouldn't, but several times she had driven by the house with the horse and buggy, always in the daylight. She secretly was just a little scared but enjoyed both the tiny shiver of fear and the knowledge of her disobedience.

One cool fall day Clara's parents sent her to town close to chore time to get various things from the general store. There were several customers ahead of her and she got to talking to Otto, a neighbor boy about her age. When she finally picked up her packages and loaded them into the buggy, the sun was just starting to drop behind the heavily wooded hillside. She set the horse to an easy trot and headed for home.

Without her really planning it, she was suddenly near the house. The big, two-story house had many windows, and the last rays of the sun reflected a wavy red in the handmade glass panes. Brush obscured the porch to one side but no brush or grass grew around the front of the house. Clara could clearly see the row of basement windows and the outside, almost flat entrance leading down into the limestone foundation.

Some force made Clara stop the buggy and get out. The wind picked up and the horse was restless, stamping and whinnying. An old iron fence with a series of spiked tops surrounded the house. Clara approached the house slowly, eyes fastened on the shining red windows and especially the lower basement windows, turning from red to black as the sun continued to drop. Her hand touched the gate, which looked rusty and felt very cold. It swung open smoothly and quietly, no sound coming from the rusty hinges. Clara hesitated. Everything she knew and believed told her to stop, but she seemed unable to control her body. She walked through, toward the basement door. Vaguely, she could hear the horse running away. She stood above the basement entrance and closed her eyes. In that instant, she knew if she lifted the door to the basement, she would never come back.

Without warning, a strong arm pulled her back, dragging her away from the house. She felt as if pulled in two, a force pulling her back to the house and a powerful body pulling her away. The body yelled several times and then the force let go. When she opened her eyes, she was on the street again, the gate shut, the house completely dark, and the wind blowing stronger still, like the beginnings of the tornado they'd had last year.

Looking up, Clara saw Otto kneeling beside her. Speaking in German, he asked her if she was hurt. She slowly shook her head from side to side.

"Why did you come? What happened?" she asked.

Looking less frightened, Otto spoke in English this time. "I was following you to be sure you came home safely. When your horse ran past me, I knew you had trouble. I came to look and found you standing here, about to go in. Why were you here? It is a dangerous place for you."

Clara looked down, embarrassed. "I don't really know. I—well, I've driven by here before and I just found myself here."

"Do you know the story about the witch?" Otto asked.

"I know my parents told me to stay away and said there was a witch who used to live here."

"Come to my wagon. I will tell you the story."

Otto helped her stand up and walked her to his wagon. Once there, he resumed his story. "The woman who lived here before was dreadfully afraid to die. My parents say she was a witch, but even witches can die. She wanted to live forever. But the only way she could keep on living was to find another body, since hers was worn out and old."

Clara shuddered. "Is she still there?"

Otto looked at her solemnly and continued. "Many years ago she did finally die. Since then she has been looking for a body. She tries to lure young girls to her basement. If she can get a young girl to come to her basement, she will take her body and be young again. That is why parents tell their daughters to stay away. I could help you because she does not want men."

Clara knew the reason for her feeling now. The feeling that told her if she went into the basement she would be lost forever. She smiled weakly at Otto as she said, "Let's go home. I promise I will never come here again."

Charley's Ghost

Charley's ghost wasn't really Charley's ghost—rather, it wasn't the ghost of Charley. But because it was Charley Nelson and his family who were most affected by the phenomenon, it came to be referred to as "Charley's ghost."

The Nelsons had come up to Iowa County from the South in about 1923, according to Jess Bean of Williamsburg. The family consisted of Charley and his wife, their son Gordon who was Jess's age, and daughter Mary who was four or five years older than Gordon.

Charley's job was to shovel coal into raised hoppers for the steam engines on the railroad. That's why they lived in a remodeled boxcar that sat across from the depot. Except for a crawl space under it, it sat right on the ground, without any wheels. There was a door at each end for easy entrance and exit.

Jess Bean was nine or ten then. He and Gordon Nelson were pals, and their fathers became acquainted, too. Jess's father, William T. Bean, was the security guard around supplies that came in on the railroad and were stacked near the depot, to be used for putting in the pavement around Williamsburg. So Mr. Bean and Mr. Nelson saw each other frequently and came to know each other quite well. The two men used to go hunting together, and they played poker with some of the same friends.

That's why it was Jess's father to whom Charley went one day to report that sometimes when the family went to bed, something would scratch on the outside of their boxcar home and keep them awake. With no trees around their home, they knew it wasn't branches. And sometimes, he said, whatever it was would knock on the outside walls.

The depot and the boxcar had been painted a dull gray. When the men went to examine the boxcar to look for the results of the scratchings, they saw shiny, swirly circles on the exterior walls, something like the swirls in fancy penmanship. But when they checked the mud after a rain, or the fresh snow in winter, there never were any strange tracks in it. So it seemed to Charley that they must have a ghost that liked to haunt them.

Charley said, "At first the ghost only showed up at night when we didn't have any lights on. When we did have light, it came from our kerosene lamp. It wasn't long before the ghost got braver and started to show up when the lamp was lit, too."

Jess said later on, "My dad tried to help Charley get rid of whatever it was that was bothering them. One night, Dad carried a revolver and asked Charley and his family if it would be all right if he shot right through the wall if the scratching persisted."

Jess explained, "Dad figured if it was anyone else trying to give them a fright or just pester them or watch them, a shot would scare him away.

"Dad was inside with his gun. He and the Nelsons were all listening. Dad hoped to aim at a spot near where the scratching sounds were made. When the scratching started again, Dad alerted the Nelsons that he was going to shoot. He did, and the noises stopped. When the men went out there, they didn't see anyone or anything suspect. But the sounds started up again half an hour later, so the men didn't think it was anyone that lived around there and was just playing around. No sane man would return after being shot at."

Charley's ghost acquired a name all its own, too. Jess told the story of how that happened.

"One night Gordon, who was interested in Model T Fords, was listening to the scratching on the wall. At that time the family didn't know that the ghost could think, but Gordon got the idea to give it sort of a test. He said, 'Make like a Model T going uphill.'

"Charley's ghost started rapping kind of slow," Jess said. "Then it slowed down some more, and just as if the Model T had reached the top of a hill and started down the other side, it gradually increased the tempo. By that, Gordon knew it could think or had some form or measure of intelligence. Then he asked it if it could understand two knocks for YES and three knocks for NO. Right away, it knocked twice to signify that it understood. That's how it came about that we could 'talk' to it," Jess finished.

After that, at any chance the boys had, when they heard the scratchings or the rappings, they tried talking to it. One of the first questions they asked was, "Are you dead?"

Immediately came two knocks for YES.

In answer to, "Were you a carpenter in your real life?" the boys heard three knocks for NO.

Another question was, "Are you a Protestant?"

The answer came as three knocks.

"Are you a Lutheran?"

Three knocks. NO.

"Are you a Catholic?"

YES.

They figured by answers to other questions that it was the ghost of a dead Irish peddler. That's why they started calling him "Irish."

Other people "talked" to Irish, too. Mostly they were friends of the Nelson family or people that Jess and his father knew. They heard the answers: the two knocks for YES and the three for NO. And if the question required an answer in small numbers, one knock meant one year or one month or day, or one item, etc.

Anyone who came into the home could ask questions. Jess said, "When my brother was only five, someone told him to ask Irish a question. William, my brother, asked, 'How many fish are there in Old Man's Creek?' Irish couldn't answer a question like that with his YES or NO answers, so he just made a series of quick rappings. Maybe that meant 'Many fish.' We weren't sure."

Jess said, "Some other people who heard Irish were the then mayor of Williamsburg, the newspaper editor, the priest, my own father and mother, and my uncle."

Then Jess continued, "This all happened over seventy years ago, right here in Williamsburg. There was another house in Iowa County, too. It was the second place the Nelsons lived, also in Williamsburg. It was just half a block off of the square. It's gone now. But the rappings on the outside walls were heard there. I myself heard them quite a few times at both places."

People would sit on the high school lawn across from that house on warm summer nights just to listen. They could hear Charley's voice when he was asking Irish questions, and they could hear Irish's knocks in answer.

There were other questions Irish could answer. For example, he could tell whether one of the poker players had a good hand, or which prizefighter was favored to win the next fight. You could usually bank on his having the right answers, and some of the poker players got disgusted and quit playing when Irish ruined their game.

Apparently a dead Irish peddler had been buried at the site where the boxcar living quarters were set down along the Chicago, Milwaukee and St. Paul railroad yard. Gordon and Jess checked out the crawl space under the boxcar once, but they couldn't find any bones or any other indication of a burial there. But maybe they didn't go deep enough.

Jess went on with his story. "My father and my Uncle Wallace even contacted a ghostbuster out of New York City. The locals had put together a pot of money. It totaled $5,000. Needless to say, the man went through the attic at the second place and mumbled something about radios and ventriloquism, but he couldn't explain anything clearly. He went back to New York City at his own expense."

Charley could get free passes for himself and his family because he worked for the railroad. When his mother-in-law died in another state, though, Charley wouldn't let his wife take the free pass and go down south to bury her. After that, Irish claimed to be the ghost of the mother-in-law, maybe giving Charley a hard time for not letting his wife go down to her own mother's funeral.

Later on, Mrs. Nelson passed away in their second home in town, that same house owned by Jess's father. Jess said that the daughter, Mary, moved away and married and the son, Gordon, lives in another state. He said that Charley left town, too.

Jess wrapped his story up with this emphasis: "I don't want the story of Charley's ghost to die with me. All of this really happened. It's not just a figment of my imagination."

Checking *on the* Help

(none of the names used in this story are real names)

If you become aware of enough eerie experiences, you might draw the conclusion that there is a ghost or a spirit around. It seems that could happen in almost any setting.

In an eastern Iowa group home for adolescent boys, several events happened within two months' time in the middle of the winter of 1991–92, and all in the middle of the night.

Most of these things happened to substitute staff members who were there for only one night at that time. After their experiences, most of them said they didn't want to be called as a sub again. Especially not at night.

But even one member of the regular staff had things happen to her. Janine said, "I walked up to the kitchen and heard a door shut firmly. I thought it odd, so I went back and walked up there again. I heard the door shut again. It sounded like the office doors, but they were locked. I checked all the doors. I couldn't figure out why a door had shut twice as I walked up to the kitchen."

Janine continued, "Since others had told of similar experiences, I wasn't really scared and I didn't draw any conclusions at the time.

"Earlier, Jim had heard a door slam, too. He was the only staff member in the house that night. The boys were all asleep. Jim said, 'It couldn't have been any human that slammed that door that night.'

"I figured we had a spirit who visited the house, or lived there, and was checking out the temporary help, making sure they were doing what they were supposed to and were taking good care of the boys. The substitutes found these incidents frightening, and they didn't want to work here again; I wasn't frightened," Janine reported.

"When it happened to me," she said, "I figured the spirit was telling me to stay at my station and not walk around in the house. Another time, I was sitting at my desk right by the bathroom when I heard the bath mat being jerked off the rail in the shower. It sounded like someone was pulling the bath mat's suction cups off the metal rail it usually hangs on next to the shower stall. When I went in to check on it, the mat was lying on the floor of the shower stall. The floor of the stall was dry.

"Another night, Bruce was reading the paper while he was working. He felt a cold breeze and felt the presence of someone he couldn't see. And Bert heard voices in the kitchen one night, but no one was in the kitchen. He also saw a shadow that formed the profile of a man on the wall, but—again—he was alone in the house, except for the boys, who were all asleep."

Janine finished her story: "We did have a boy living there that winter who had been interested in the supernatural and other than Christian rites. The eerie things stopped happening for a while after he left. We don't know if there was any connection. But just a few months ago, Tony and I were talking. He was saying, 'I'm not afraid of spirits. If I meet up with any, I'll just rebuke them in the name of the Lord.' Right after he said that, we both heard a poster rattle on the wall. So maybe we do still have a ghost there. Maybe you can come and work there and meet up with him sometime."

A Child's Spirit

The house is in West Union, not far from the Country Club. It is not a large home, only two bedrooms. But Emily remembers that the house was big enough for her family—and for an unseen guest.

When Emily and her mother lived in the little, white, one-story home, Emily was just a young girl, perhaps ten years old. Emily was an only child and was used to playing by herself. She had a vivid imagination and invented stories and friends as children often do. But one day her games became more real than pretend.

Emily had a small closet in her bedroom where she kept her few toys and clothes. One summer morning she woke up and heard a noise in her closet. Curious, she got up, still sleepy, and opened the door. The sound stopped and Emily shut the door. She thought of telling her mother, but if it was a mouse, she would try to catch it for a pet. She would make a cage to keep it safe from Abby, their dog. Abby lived outside in the doghouse, but when he came in the house he would stand by Emily's closet and whine.

The next morning she heard the noise again. She went to the closet and opened the door quickly, but the sound stopped. This time she had listened to the sound better and she did not think it was a mouse. The noise was an irregular thumping and sounded familiar. On the third morning, she stayed in bed and the thumping kept up, not loud and not mouse-like. Emily thought about the noise more, and suddenly she knew why it sounded familiar. She got up, opened the closet door, and took out her rubber ball. No sound came from the closet now. Emily bounced the rubber ball on the wooden floor by her bed. That was it! One loud thump and then several small quick thumps as the ball hit the floor rapidly and finally rolled to a stop. Someone was bouncing her ball in the closet!

Emily was not afraid. She had been vaguely aware of a feeling that someone was watching her since they had moved in. Not a bad or scary feeling—just there. She liked to play with her ball. Was there a spirit child that liked to play with her ball, too?

At dinner that day, Emily told her mother about the closet. Her mother told her she was imagining things again. But her mother also looked upset. Emily always knew because her mother's face got all tight and she pressed her lips together until they were white.

"Emily, you are making up stories again." She paused. "But if you hear that sound again, call me. And leave your door open."

"Yes, Mommy. Do you think this is a little girl like me?"

"I don't think it is anything! But call me if you hear any noises."

Emily did not hear the sound again for another week, although she put the ball back in the closet and shut the door tightly each night. Then she heard it once again and called to her mother. Her mother hurried to the room in the first faint light of dawn, hugging her robe about herself.

"Do you hear it, Mommy?"

Her mother rubbed her arms, quiet. She reached down and held Emily close to her. In a low voice she said, "Yes, Emily dear, I hear it."

Emily found her mother in her room frequently after that, looking in the closet, knocking on the walls. And she insisted that Emily keep a light on and leave the door wide open.

"But, Mommy, I'm not a baby. And I'm not scared."

"Emily, don't argue. You'll feel better."

Actually Emily thought her mother felt better with the light on.

Sometimes Emily thought she heard a faint humming or singing, but the sound was too soft to hear very well. The noises kept on and Emily got used to it. She would play with the ball in the daytime and leave it in the closet at night. The noise would start early in the morning and stop by the middle of the morning.

Several months later Emily and her mother were sitting in the living room. Her mother was knitting her another itchy wool sweater and Emily was playing with her doll, Ann. In the corner, almost behind her mother's chair, was the rocking chair Emily's grandfather had made for her. Emily could no longer fit in the chair comfortably, but she often put Ann in it. Today she put Ann in the chair and went to the kitchen.

"It's almost supper time, Emily."

"Yes, Mommy. I was just going to get some water from the bucket."

Emily came back into the living room and saw Ann rocking back and forth in the chair. She smiled. Ann was an old doll and her only doll, but still pretty with her china head and dark hair. Then Emily noticed the chair was rocking for an awfully long time.

"Mommy, did you push the rocker?"

Her mother pushed her glasses up on her nose. "What, Emily?"

"Did you push Ann in the rocking chair?"

Turning, her mother looked at the rocker. After watching the chair rock for some time, she said slowly, "No, Emily, I did not. Please take Ann out of the chair."

Emily went over and stopped the rocker, picked Ann up carefully, and straightened her skirt. She went back and sat on the sofa with her doll. Her mother had already moved there. Emily and her mother watched the chair. Very slowly, it moved slightly back and forth. Each time it went a little farther until it was rocking the same as before.

Emily was delighted. "Look, Mommy, the chair can rock."

Her mother put her arm around Emily. They watched the chair for ten or fifteen minutes, until it finally stopped rocking.

"Emily, we are going to move soon."

"But why, Mommy? I like it here."

"I don't! We'll move as soon as I can find another place."

And within a week, they did move. Emily's mother never spoke of the incidents or the house again, but Emily found out years later from an aunt that her mother felt as if she were being watched, too. Other tenants have not reported anything unusual, but maybe they have not had any little girl for the spirit child to play with.

A City of Many Ghosts

Evidently Davenport would be a good place to live if you were interested in hosting ghosts. Or if you were a ghost, you could probably join a whole company of them there.

Jim Arpy, writing for the Times-Democrat, Davenport, wrote several stories about hauntings at the old Pi Kappa Chi fraternity house on Main Street in that city. Residents of the house at the time were students at the Palmer College of Chiropractic. Arpy related some very scary incidents that took place there, including heavy footsteps being heard, locked doors opening and closing, typewriter keys striking and toilets flushing without human aid.

Arpy's May 11, 1972, story gave an account of celebrated Chicago medium Mrs. Irene Hughes' visit to the fraternity house. Hughes felt that the main spirit was that of a medical doctor who was also involved in politics. Later research revealed that a medical doctor had owned the home for a long time and had also been involved in politics. Hughes described the doctor/spirit as one who felt that he was right in most things and wanted the present occupants of the house to do things his way.

A few years later, Arpy wrote about another apparently haunted house in northwest Davenport. In this case, an adult couple were experiencing unexplainable incidents that left them frightened and puzzled. Both had been in good health when they began to remodel the old schoolhouse that became their new home; after that, both had been sick much of the time. The couple told of furniture sliding all the way across rooms, day and night. Lights and faucets mysteriously came on, seemingly by themselves; their TV and radio came on, and in general things happened that they didn't direct or initiate.

A daughter-in-law who spent some time visiting the same couple in that house fell several times as the result of what she described as a push. Dark figures were seen, loud knocks and heavy footsteps were heard, and other unexplainable things happened. Was the remodeled old schoolhouse haunted by teachers and students of earlier years? Do they return to rearrange the furnishings and set the house in order, according to their accustomed plan?

In an October 31, 1971, Times story, Arpy told about another haunted house in McClellan Heights. There, the children in one particular bedroom cried at night. When the parents went to check, they were always surrounded by a terribly cold area just outside that door—like a very cold, chilling wind they couldn't account for. When he researched, the owner found out that his house was built on land that was once part of old Camp McClellan, a Civil War training camp, and that his house was built near and possibly partly over a Native American burial ground.

A few days later, two staff writers wrote for Davenport's The Leader about a Davenport businesswoman who with her elderly parents shared a house on Main Street with "a friendly spirit named Elsie." That extra "presence" was felt both inside the house and out in the yard where she removed a lot of trees and shrubs and put in a new fence. A neighbor told the young woman that Elsie had once lived in the old house, loved it, and "spent long hours in the yard." It would seem that her presence was still being felt.

Arpy wrote of another huge old house in Davenport, this one on Ripley Street, where many young men had lived as students. The date and name of the newspaper were lost in the process of getting copies from the "Haunted House" file in the Davenport Public Library's Special Collections Room. But the article made it clear that the roomers in that house had been very frightened a number of times by various phenomena including a man's figure, a strange cat, heavy footsteps, a cold room where a presence was felt, and locked doors being found unlocked.

In The Leader of October 29, 1986, the McClellan Heights house was again featured by staff writer Rita Pearson. Another story by Michael Ashcraft featured a young couple and their first house, an old one. When they first went through it, it felt "old and sad and lonely." The couple wanted to restore an old house; "they wanted one with spirit." The one they got had windows that came open by themselves even if they were nailed shut. Apparently it had spirit enough for them. What kind of spirit is lost in the file at the Davenport library, on page C2 of that newspaper, unless, of course, the spirit itself purposely misplaced the rest of the story.

Several other ghosts "live" in Davenport. There is another house that seems to have hosted a ghost for quite some time. The house is one of the original river mansions. At the time of this writing, it was the home of Davenport Mayor Patrick Gibbs and his family. Gibbs said, "We haven't experienced any happenings, but talk with the previous owners." And so I did. But that is another story in itself.

Do Playmates Live *in* Their Upstairs?

When Jim and Judy first moved into their house in a quiet neighborhood in southwest Cedar Rapids, they didn't know it was still occupied. True—the people who sold them the house had moved out, but they hadn't told the buyers about the invisible occupants.

One evening about a year later, Judy and four-year-old Colin were visiting Judy's mother. That left Jim at home with the infant son, Hunter. While Hunter slept, Jim was reading—until such a loud noise shook the house that Jim was nearly scared out of his chair in the den. The den and the garage share a wall, which made Jim think someone had rammed a car into the side of the garage.

He didn't see anything wrong out there when he looked out the windows. He couldn't leave Hunter there alone, and he did not want to disturb his sleep, so he called 911. When the police came by, they looked around but could find nothing that would point to a crash. Jim said, "In fact, they looked at me as if they thought I had been drinking. Then as time passed, I sort of forgot about the experience."

One evening several months later, Jim got out of his chair in the den to go out to the kitchen. He explained, "The den is sunken, with two steps down into it from a small landing." Then he went on to tell what happened. "As I neared the landing, I had the sensation that a medium-sized dog had just jumped into my arms. But we don't have a dog and none appeared. Even though I had seen nothing, I had a strong mental image of the dog. It had been there, somehow. Judy saw me as I jumped back in shock, and she asked, 'Did the dog jump up on you just now?' That was when I learned that Judy had had the very same experience in the same spot in that house."

The dog incident made them think back to when they first moved in. They started wondering if the sellers were so anxious to bargain with them because of scary experiences they had had. They had left a lot of things in the house, including an upstairs bed, fully made. Jim and Judy thought that was really unusual, especially now that strange things were happening to them. And the sellers had also sold their business and left town and not stopped back since then to ask how things were going for the new occupants.

Jim remembered, too, that when his sister stopped by with a housewarming gift, he had noticed her reaction. He knew about her previous experiences with ghosts and poltergeists. He remembered that she moved quickly but thoughtfully through the house, pausing here and there, as if aware of a presence, but said nothing to them as to having sensed anything.

After the dog experience, things were pretty quiet until the 1992 Christmas holiday season. From then on, Jim said, "Our comfortable lifestyle in the home of our dreams changed dramatically."

Jim's niece Janelle and her boyfriend were with them a few nights after Christmas. Jim, Judy, their small sons Colin and Hunter, and Janelle and her guest were all in the den watching movies when Jim and Janelle heard the door to the upstairs stairway open and close. Though the door is in a different part of the house, they recognized its distinctive sound. Realizing that all the people in the house were right there in the den, the adults investigated, only to find the door "solidly shut," as Jim put it.

More experiences started to surface. Janelle stopped by the next night to tell about what had happened to her the summer before, while she was housesitting for them. That same door had actually opened and closed one night while she was there alone. Though she had had some "bad vibes," as she put it, before that, she had said nothing. Jim said, "Janelle is a very independent, confident twenty-one-year-old used to living alone in her apartment. She isn't easily frightened, but she was that weekend here, alone. She ended up sleeping on the couch, while the door opened and closed on its own several times that night. She tried to blame it on a draft."

After the December repetition of her experience, it seemed that it occurred whenever Janelle came by. Jim said, "We consulted experts. They suggested one, that it could be the ghost of a boy who might be 'flirting' with Janelle, or two, that Janelle and I together create some type of energy that triggers supernatural happenings in the house."

On New Year's Eve, Janelle and her girlfriend Bobbi stopped by to celebrate. That night, after the boys were asleep in bed, the adults were watching rented movies and playing some games when suddenly they all looked at each other as they realized there was someone else in the den with them—a presence or a spirit that they each knew was there, though they actually saw nothing physical.

As Jim made an attempt to describe it, he said, "The presence moved in a half-moon configuration from one doorway to the other, and a cold draft absolutely filled the room. We sat tight in our chairs, but I finally got up enough nerve to leave my chair and describe my sensation to the others. They all felt the same type of movement, as though all of us sensed exactly the same thing but none of us saw anything real that could be described easily.

"We moved from the den into the front living room in the other part of the house. At that point we all became extremely frightened. Janelle described the spirit as actually standing over her, touching her. Yet no one saw anything! She sat and sobbed for the rest of the evening, and we all stayed up until nearly 4 a.m., scared to pieces! When midnight came, we didn't even think about wishing each other a happy new year!

Do Playmates Live in Their Upstairs?   *37*

"We think the spirit 'lives' in our upstairs and that there is also a presence in our basement. My sister thinks so, too."

Jim said that he and Judy were both puzzled. In fact, they were frightened enough that each of them started waiting outside for the other after work, until they could both go in together. They even adjusted their work schedules so they could leave at the same time each morning.

They were both truly afraid, even though they didn't feel that the presence or presences represented evil or the Devil at all. It was just so strange. They wished the contacts with the spirit or spirits would end. At night, they closed their bedroom door and pulled the covers up to their chins, yet were afraid and were unable to sleep. Some nights they were up all night, meanwhile trying not to say anything that would scare the boys.

But they soon learned that Hunter had already known something was different there. When he was three, he burst into their bedroom one Saturday morning with a very strange look on his face. "He truly looked possessed," Jim said. "We followed him out to the living room. Hunter was frantic. While he tried to open the upstairs door so he could go up there, he was all the while yelling, 'Kids, come back! Kids, come back!'

"Hunter appeared to be sleepwalking. When we got him fully awake and talked about it later, he told us that three boys, all older than he is, 'live' in our upstairs. He thought they were maybe about six, eight, and twelve. Hunter said that at night they all come down to the boys' room. They want to play with their toys. Sometimes they're hungry, too. He said they all sleep in our upstairs in our king-size bed sometimes, and they come from the house next door through our attic, into our upstairs, and down into his and Colin's room.

"We know all about young children having very active imaginations, and we know sometimes children have imagined playmates they talk to, but this was something different. We saw it in Hunter's face as he tried to open that door and get the kids to come back. It seemed so real to us that we checked into who actually lives next door, but there are no children living there at this time.

"After learning about Hunter's experiences, we feel certain that the spirits living in our home are the spirits of children. Hunter also says that sometimes at night their Daddy drives them to our house to drop them off to play. Sometimes he even stands in the doorway to our boys' room and watches them play. That made us wonder if the garage/car crash sound was related. But how could it be?

"We contacted two professional exorcists," Jim said. "One of them suggested lighting white or light-colored candles and doing prayer rituals. We did that as a group of three adults—the two of us and Janelle. The other exorcist suggested hanging pictures of Jesus Christ throughout our home to protect us from potential evil. We tried that, too, although no one believes our entity to be evil. We feel that our ghost or ghosts are friendly, and since the 'weird' things tend to happen at holiday time, we believe positive experiences such as a holiday trigger their behavior."

Jim and Judy finally contacted some of the former owners of the home to ask if they had had any experiences like theirs. The family they had bought the house from were evasive, but did admit to finding the house "full of religious paraphernalia." They said they removed all of it and burned it. The man said that a few things had been left in the attic, but he had been afraid to go up there to get them, "so maybe they're still there."

The man's wife said the only thing she ever felt weird about was the trim along the entire length of the front of the house. The trim was made up of unusual shapes—stars and circles carved into a decorative strip, and painted the same as the house. Jim and Judy had noticed it, but hadn't paid much attention to it.

The former housewife also told them that one time a stranger stopped by, rang the doorbell, and told them they should get out of the house because of those shapes, "those evil signs." But then, she also said she didn't believe the person enough to act on the warning.

Before that couple lived there, the occupants were grandparents of some of Jim and Judy's co-workers. They checked to find out if there were any weird incidents then, but only found out that the home was always filled with love and that holidays were a special time. Yet, they learned that each of those two elderly occupants had died at separate times in that same house, in the room where Hunter claims to host visitors and in the bed where the two boys sleep.

"We don't exactly know where to go from here," Jim said. "We love our home, but we don't feel totally comfortable with what's happening. Sometimes we feel perfectly safe. Then something else happens, and we're unsure.

"During the most trying weeks when we were almost afraid even to come home at night, Judy and I finally got out one day just for a chance to relax for a few hours' drive. The boys were with Janelle at her apartment. We had stayed home so much, just to avoid the fear upon returning, that it felt really good to get away and relax once.

"When Judy and I went back home, Janelle hadn't brought the boys back yet. We sat down in the den, still feeling more comfortable and relaxed than we had for a long time, when a huge moan came from the corner of the den. Someone or something moaned once, then again about ten seconds later. I was more scared than ever before. I thought I'd have a heart attack and die right then and there. If I hadn't been barefoot, I believe I would have run out the door and abandoned the place. But there was deep snow outside. We tried to convince ourselves that the noise had come through the flue of the fireplace, or from an electronic toy, but we knew it didn't. We both heard it, experienced it.

"That same week, we were called to a friend's house on an emergency. Janelle and her boyfriend came to babysit the boys. When Judy and I returned, the young couple were huddled together in absolute terror in a corner of the kitchen. What had frightened them so? They told us that while they were in the den, the electronics in the house—the VCR, stereo, lights, everything—had gone bonkers, all these things turning themselves on and off. The two couldn't abandon the children (they were in bed), so they waited in absolute fear for us to come back. Janelle's boyfriend never did come back to our house.

"I can't blame him a bit. Even though we think of our ghosts, or whatever they are, as friendly spirits, I'm home alone as I write this down for you—and it's giving me the goose bumps even as I write."

Does Herb Still Watch Out ℱℴ𝓇 His House?

One could say, "It happens to the best of us" or "It even happens to college presidents"—It being the phenomenon of strange happenings such as those that occurred at the home of the president of Teikyo Westmar University at Le Mars in 1993, when this story was written.

Joe Olander and his wife Cheryl lived in a house they think was built in the 1890s by Herbert Martin, a former Le Mars attorney. Officials of the college (then Western Union College) bought the house from Martin's family in the early 1930s, according to an article in the Le Mars Daily Sentinel of June 25, 1993.

In her article, staff writer Cassie Kinney wrote that even the earlier presidents of the college saw and heard things they couldn't explain easily. When the Olanders arrived, they were told about these past happenings by a previous Teikyo Westmar president and his wife.

It wasn't long before the nightly footsteps and the window closings started when Joe was out of town—in fact, out of the country. Imagine how Cheryl Olander must have felt when she heard the loud footsteps on the wooden attic stairs, or found the window closed—"every night," Joe Olander said, "while I was gone." No doubt once would be enough, for most folks. The same incidents repeated nightly could drive many rightful occupants out of the house.

Herb is what Joe called the "presence" in their house, named so for Herbert Martin who is considered to be a likely reason behind the strange occurrences. Joe thinks Herb sort of continued to look after the house he built, even though he died in 1941.

Some folks think Martin returned to the house he once lost (along with his life's assets and the respect of the people) because he didn't really want to leave it. Another June 25, 1993, Daily Sentinel article about Martin states that although he had been respected by other attorneys, his involvement in farm foreclosures in the 1930s changed his life drastically. He was not the same after a large crowd of farmers "rushed" him and threatened his life. Whatever the reason, it seems that for many years after Herb Martin died, his spirit lingered in his former home.

A part of the legend that has built up around Herbert Martin and his house is that he also protected it from burglaries, twice, by showing up at the right moment and scaring away the would-be robbers by his "lifelike" appearance.

And other things have happened, according to the Olanders. Once, when Cheryl was leaving the house, she thought of something she had forgotten. Once back inside, she heard someone running up the attic steps. Up there in the attic, there was nothing except a closet in a corner. Joe thinks the closet may have been the place Herb had chosen for his little world, or afterworld, if you wish. But he also made his presence known in the basement, where there was a wine cellar. He chose to set bottles upright that were laid horizontally in the wine racks. Joe said that things kept on happening."One other thing was that when we came home, curtains we had left down would be up—or those we left up would be down. It happened often."

Joe also believed that the "character" he called Herb played with their answering machine. I could agree, there. When I first tried to contact the Olanders by telephone, I heard just two rings, then an ordinary beginning of a message: "We are unable to come to the phone." Then silence. And finally, "name and number." The next time I tried, later the same day, I heard brief parts of the message, then a "beep," then nothing. I wasn't sure I wanted to leave a message, if it was Herb on the line, so I hung up and called later that day. Joe was home by then.

Joe thinks that "we are either spiritual beings with a physical body, or we are physical bodies with a spiritual dimension. And I believe," he continued, "that we are spiritual beings that have a physical body, and when our physical body dies our spirit goes on living."

That is how Joe explains Herb, if he can be explained at all: though his physical body is dead, Herb's spirit goes on living—in the home at 935 Fourth Avenue Southeast in Le Mars.

The Olanders weren't afraid of Herb, as long as he was a good ghost—a watchful, protective one. It must have been like having someone around to keep them company when the house was a little too quiet.

A Dog of a Ghost

When you live in a house for a time, you develop a feel for the place. Or maybe you feel a presence there. Sometimes it takes the form of a person, sometimes the form of an object or animal. That's the way Becky told it.

"When I was a girl," she said, "I lived near Spillville in a house that had a ghost. My sister and I both knew it, but our mother wouldn't let us talk about it. Maybe she didn't want to encourage the ghost. Or us.

"In another house I lived in, there were collectibles and antiques, including some unusual dolls. I felt a presence there, too. I'd see something in a mirror, but when I'd look again, there'd be nothing there. Once I saw a young woman's figure in the doorway. She was the perfect image of an older woman I knew had died, but she appeared in her younger being. I would hear the clip-clop of the sandals she used to wear. It almost seemed as if she wasn't quite ready to give up the life she knew there. She seemed to hang around a lot. Once, she walked right past the bed and through the wall. After that, she was gone.

"Someone said that maybe death occurrences were being reflected in these happenings." Becky went on to explain. "A long time ago, a hired man died in that house. Years later, someone wearing farmer's boots constantly made footsteps on the roof. Something made noises in a closet at night. In the mornings, when we opened that closet, all the clothes would be on the floor."

Becky said that was the closet where the old dolls had been stored. "I remember one doll," she said, "that had vibrant blue eyes. I couldn't help but notice them. I always had a feeling that doll would come to life and move toward me and talk to me. It was after the dolls were in there for a long time that the sounds started coming from the closet."

One more incident came to Becky from the years she spent in that house. "Coming home at night," she recalled, "we'd see lights on in the attic. And one night while we were watching TV in the living room, a hurricane lamp on a table by the window raised up a foot, then crashed down and broke with no apparent reason. In another room, on another night, another hurricane lamp exploded, again with no reasonable explanation."

"Whatever was behind these incidents, there were more," Becky went on. "We moved again, and this time it was to a house north of Decorah. That's where the strange presence took the form of a dog. By then, I had two sons. When Jimmy, my older boy, was about a year old, he could talk pretty well. He knew the word 'puppy' and he'd say 'puppy' for any dog he saw, anywhere. He'd even wake up in the night screaming 'Puppy! Puppy!' This went on for about a year. Sometimes in the daytime he'd scramble up the stairs from the first floor, and between breaths he'd be hollering, 'Mommy! Mommy! Puppy after me!'

"One night, I let him sleep in my bed. When I heard my younger boy crying that night, I let him cry a little rather than wake Jimmy by my getting up. Of course, I was hoping the baby would go back to sleep. But he didn't, and I thought I'd better go see why he was crying. I sat up, and there at the end of the bed was a huge black Labrador with luminous golden eyes staring at Jimmy still asleep in my bed. Those eyes were more than bright or shining. Some weird kind of light seemed to be coming right out of them, toward Jimmy. They projected an expression of intelligence, yet evil.

"That scared me into action. I kicked hard at the dog, and just that fast it was gone. It had been there, though—not a reflection in the mirror, not a dream. It was the biggest Labrador I've ever seen. In that one close-up look in the dim light from the hall, I saw its ears hanging close to its head. I saw the long, powerful jaws and its black, dense coat and those penetrating gold eyes.

"Though I spent anxious minutes wondering if that was the last of it, Jimmy never said 'Puppy!' again to let me know he'd seen it. He never even seemed to dream about it. When he was a little older, we talked about it. I asked him if he'd ever seen one in the house or in his room since those other times, and his answer was 'No.' In the years that followed, he was never dogged by that ghost again."

Dust and Green Stones

When Ricky was just a little boy, he lived up on the ridges south of Guttenberg, out of the valley of the city, on a farm with his mother and brothers and sisters. His father had died a year ago and it was a struggle, but they were making a living.

Ricky was small for his age. Although he was eight and could cultivate with the horses, he still had the dustiest, dirtiest job reserved for the smallest person: tying baling wire for the baler. But when Ricky's chores were done, he loved to explore the hills and caves and creeks in the area. Since his siblings were all much older, Ricky usually made his expeditions alone. Sometimes he walked but usually took the old mare and rode around the wooded bluffs and hills.

The day he remembers so well was a fall day, and Indian summer day with bright sunshine. The leaves had drifted from the trees and made a vivid rustling carpet in the woods. Although Ricky's mother had warned him many times about staying close to home, he was already several miles away on this day. He was going to explore the huge wooded bluff on the south side. The road was steep and treacherous and impassable in spring and winter. It was not far from Miner's Creek, so named by Daniel Justice, who started the first lead mine here.

Ricky had been up and down Miner's Creek, looking for—and sometimes finding—old lead shafts. But on the wooded bluff he headed for today, he had found caves both large and small. He had been here just last week and found several small openings and one large shallow cave. He had also seen a small opening behind some brush, but had no time to explore since it was getting dark. He liked exploring caves. He had found several arrowheads and once, a large stone he took home. His mother told him it was a hide scraper, used to remove the flesh from a hide so it could be cured and used. Ricky had found several stone axes, too, and kept them in a special drawer with his rattlesnake skins.

Searching the ground carefully, Ricky found the small opening from the week before. He tied his mare to a tree and, kneeling, pushed the prickly gooseberry bushes away from the opening. He had almost missed it last week because of them. Carefully, Ricky pushed a stick into the opening and slid it back and forth, checking for and rattlesnakes. His family had lost two cattle to rattlesnakes last year.

Satisfied, he squeezed into the opening and started wriggling through the tunnel ahead. The tunnel was cool but not wet, as many were. He crawled a long time and stopped, wondering if he should turn back. What if a rock fell on him? No one would know where he was. What if a rattlesnake bit him now? His old mare would never make it home before he died from the poison. He started sniffing and wiped his nose on his sleeve. Well, maybe he'd just crawl a few more feet and then squeeze himself tight into a ball and turn around.

Soon, he thought the tunnel was getting a little bigger and wider. His head didn't bump the top now. Gradually, the tunnel became large enough for him to stand up. Ricky pulled out the wooden matches he had taken from the match holder and an old candle. His mother would be angry if she knew he had them, but he had watched her many times and would be careful. Using a dry stone from his pocket, he struck the match and lit the candle.

He was in a large cave. It was not as big as his mother's kitchen, but bigger than any cave he had seen. It was drier than the other caves he had been in, too. He slowly looked around, shadows flickering on the walls as he turned. There were small objects scattered here and there. When he had almost completed his circle, he noticed a bundle in the corner. He tentatively walked toward it and saw it was a tattered blanket, reddish brown with a design in yellow. Ricky leaned forward slightly and then jerked back. There were bony feet and a hand sticking out from under the blanket! Breathing quickly, he said in a quavering voice, "Hello?" No answer, no movement. Again Ricky approached slowly, ready to run and jump in the tunnel. Holding the candle up high, he saw the brown hands and feet, thinner than even his bedridden Uncle Jack's. His eyes traveled up the blanked to the brown, shrunken, face. Frightened, he ran to the tunnel entrance, wanting to get away from this silent, spooky, place with the shadows flickering on the wall. But then he remembered when he had been scared before his father died. His father told him he had to be brave. Taking a deep breath, Ricky haltingly approached what he now realized was a skeleton with skin stretched over it.

Cautiously, he looked down and saw straight, black hair. Edging slightly closer, he saw that the hair was in braids. Inching even closer, he could see that just under the ghastly shriveled chin was a necklace with green stones. The stones had holes in them and were roughly rounded. Evenly spaced from the center were two larger pieces of flat, oblong green stone. Ricky noticed small pots and arrowheads around the body and further away, pieces of what might have been arrows and a bow.

He looked back at the necklace. The wire glinted when the candle moved. He set the candle away from the face, which changed in the light and looked now as if it was smiling grimly at him. None of the men Ricky knew wore necklaces; this must be a special man.

Ricky wanted to touch the necklace, but he didn't want to touch the ghastly, grinning body. Holding his breath, he leaned toward the necklace. Just as his small hand gently touched the necklace, he lost his balance and fell forward, right into the grinning face. He screamed as he hit the body and his screams echoed around the cave, over and over. The skeleton man crumpled under him. Ricky scrambled away from the body, tipping the candle over in his haste. The candle snuffed out.

Still screaming and now crying, he groped wildly about the cave until he found the tunnel. It seemed to be a very long time before he saw the light and wriggled free. Tripping and falling, he ran to his mare, clambered on her back and kicked her toward home.

Ricky's mother called him several times for dinner and he did not come down. Finally, in a mixture of exasperation and concern, she went upstairs to his room. She found him huddled under his quilt, crying and gripping a necklace strung with green stones.

His brothers and sisters did not believe Ricky's story, although his mother assured him that she did. Ricky never went back to the cave again. When the new highway was put in down the south Guttenberg hill, the construction crew had to dynamite much of the wooded hill. With the dynamite went the cave and the bones. But Ricky still has the necklace of green stones.

An Eerie Feeling

There's an old saying: "He died with his boots on." Did it originally refer to a soldier, or a cowboy? In one very recent case, that comment came close to applying to a woman from Spirit Lake. However, she is still very much alive, so I'll change the saying to "She slept with her boots on—almost!"

The woman's name is Elda Lynn. Elda believes it pays to be cautious. Elda is even older now, and she wants to be able to move as fast as possible when she needs to. She also knows that the house she lives in all alone is very old.

Just in case of a fire, Elda keeps a coat, boots, and a warm cap handy near the door. "The boots," she says, "are just in case I have to hit a snow bank fast." She added, "I have a northeast bedroom. I have to walk through the bathroom to get to the kitchen. And I have to walk right over the top of where the furnace is in the basement, too, if I leave by the north door. When it gets very cold out, I worry about what to do if a fire starts in the old house. So, just in case, I keep a warm coat, a pair of snow boots, and a warm cap there by the north door."

One more safety measure Elda took was to buy a flashlight that can be set upright on the floor and still have the room lit up, if the electricity is off. "I figured it would help me get to the wraps and find the key and doorknob faster than in the dark," she explained.

After she got the flashlight, Elda decided one night she ought to try it out so she would be familiar with how it worked, just in case she ever had to get out in a hurry. She set it on the kitchen floor, turned off the only other light she had on, and turned on the flashlight. "It lit the room up real nice," she said. Then she turned it off, made sure both doors were locked, and went to bed.

That was December of 1992. The weatherman forecasted extremely cold temperatures that night, but Elda was ready for that.

Elda said, "I don't always fall asleep right away. Sometimes I lie there with my eyes opening and closing for several hours. That night, every time I dozed off, a noise would wake me. I thought there was someone trying to break in, until I remembered the forecast. Then I decided the old house was creaking from the dropping temperatures. That made me think about fires and how serious they could be in very cold weather.

"It was about midnight when I opened my eyes once more, only to be surprised by a light coming from another room. I had not heard the door lock click, or a doorknob turn, or any other sound just then, so I lay there quietly for a few minutes trying to decide what to do. I wasn't really scared, but I was sure puzzled. I live on the first floor of the house, but no one lives upstairs. There I was, all alone. At least nothing was too far away, including the door, whatever or whoever was there.

"I didn't turn any lights on when I got out of bed. I could see well enough by the street light to feel my way to the living room, but nothing was different there from when I had checked the doors.

"I went on around the corner to the kitchen, where I found lots of light. There was my new flashlight, sitting up straight on the floor and lighting up the whole room. I reached down and turned it off. It hadn't tipped over or anything. It had somehow come on all by itself—or had it?

"It was a pretty eerie feeling I had then, as I went back to bed with my stomach churning and tried to get back to sleep. I found myself thinking about how very old the house is and wondering what logical explanation there could be for such an unexplainable incident. I began in my mind to try to guess what the history of the house was, before I moved there. Had someone died there? Had someone fallen down the stairs in the dark, the stairs I never use, and come back to make sure there was a light available for me? Even when I was asleep?"

Elizabeth's Still Wondering

It was a Monday in February of 1956. That was the day when something happened at both ends of the day, and Elizabeth is still wondering if the two were somehow connected.

It was a stressful time for her neighbors' family: their nineteen-year-old daughter Agnes was losing a struggle with cancer.

On that morning, the first thing that happened was that Agnes died there in the family's home on the farm on Coon Creek in the southern part of Benton County. News of Agnes's death spread quickly through the small town nearby and through the school.

But Elizabeth was the first person to know. She knew the minute it happened. She said, "I had sat up by her bedside all night, Sunday the nineteenth and in the early hours of Monday the twentieth. As the sun came up bright and beautiful that morning, Agnes sat up in bed. Then she looked out the window and spoke the only words she had uttered in months. She announced, 'The sun is coming up.'"

After a brief pause, Elizabeth continued. "I stayed at her bedside that morning while the family did their chores and had their breakfast. I knew that Agnes's father Alex was sitting in the kitchen reading the daily paper and her mother Carolyn was in the cellar, washing up the separator. So I stayed with Agnes.

"Later that same morning, I was still sitting by her bedside when the 'Grim Reaper' came for her. Agnes took one long breath. The next one was a little shorter, and the third one was her last.

"I was right there, watching so she wouldn't hurt herself if she struggled. But all of us gathered around the bed by then watched her go quietly. We knew her pain and her suffering were over. The priest had been called; he came out and blessed her before the body was taken from the home."

The girl's struggle was over and arrangements would be made by the family, so Elizabeth left their home and walked about a quarter of a mile up the road to her own home. As she would have expected at that time of the morning, her husband was away at work and their three children were at school, in town. As she entered the quiet house, she wondered if the kids had heard the news already, there at the school.

After a little lunch, Elizabeth went back to her neighbors' home to clean and, in general, put the house in order. There was still the rest of the family to consider; Agnes had left three sisters and a brother, in addition to her parents.

About four o'clock, before their mother returned home, Elizabeth's children stepped off the school bus at their own gate. As they entered their own home an unexplainable incident took place. Right there, in their own living room.

At first, everything looked normal to the kids. The antique bookcase and writing desk were in their places across the corner of the living room. Nothing else seemed to be awry, either. But suddenly the glass in the door of the bookcase broke. It shattered into thousands of little pieces, some shards falling inside toward and among the books, and others falling outward onto the rug.

A little later, when Elizabeth came home and saw the scattered, splintered glass, she didn't understand at first what had happened. It was only a natural reaction to ask, "Who broke it?" But the kids had such honest, yet puzzled looks on their faces when they answered that their mother believed they had had nothing to do with it. "It just happened," they told her.

Now Elizabeth asked herself some questions: Why would the glass in the door break suddenly? Why on that particular day? No one had done anything to shatter the glass of the door that way. Had the spirit of Agnes who died just a short way down the road that morning put in an appearance at the neighbors'? Was her spirit reluctant to experience such an early ending? Or was it a death rap or an omen?

Elizabeth is still wondering: If there was a connection between the two events of that day, what was it?

Fredrica May Have Moved to Fisher

Numerous references in Iowa State University publications and in Ames city newspapers easily lead one to believe that there was, or perhaps is, indeed a ghost of the school's theater buildings. In fact, it seems that the ghost, formerly occupying Shattuck Theater, moved on to the new Fisher Theater, once Shattuck was demolished.

Shattuck was originally built on the Ames campus in 1900 as a stock judging pavilion (sometimes sheep, sometimes horses). It was a gray, round, frame structure located near the Landscape Architecture and the Journalism buildings. In 1931, when it was redone, it became the home of the Iowa State Players and was used as a theater workshop until 1973 when Fisher Theater was ready for use.

Iowa State Players had been established by Fredrica V. Shattuck shortly after she came to ISU in 1914 as the first director of theater on campus. At first, the building was called the theater workshop. Articles state that it was not easy to establish dramatics in the technical school, but Fredrica was interested, and she worked enthusiastically to do that.

In 1960, the building was renamed Shattuck Theater in her honor. She had retired in 1948, and she died in 1969. That's when folks who have been on the campus and in theater say strange things began to occur there.

Professors who had directed plays and students who performed in them or helped with sets, lighting, etc. were not happy to hear that Shattuck would be torn down, but it was deteriorating and restoration would be too costly. Perhaps they were not the only ones who would miss it. It seems that, although the students could work there on productions with very little supervision, they hesitated to be there alone, especially at night. They thought it had a ghost.

Perhaps it did. Perhaps it was the ghost of Fredrica Shattuck.

Articles from the Special Collections/Archives of the Iowa State University Library relate numerous instances of encounters with a ghost in the stock judging pavilion-turned-theater. One student reported outside doors opening on a snowy evening, when all doors were locked. Then came the sound of footsteps followed by a door closing. But there were no tracks out in the snow other than that student's own footprints as he had entered.

Sherry Hoopes, a former ISU speech professor who had also directed several plays, took part with others in a seance in the theater. As they did, though nothing else noteworthy happened, the group all had the feeling that someone was watching them.

A group of students rehearsing late one night heard sounds above them, on the stage. When they went up to check, they saw a wheelchair cross the stage to center and come to a halt facing the audience, in monologue position. It was Fredrica's old wooden wheelchair. She had used it in her later years, after she had suffered a stroke, before her death. It had been kept as a prop after her death. But who had pushed it across the stage into that position? None of the students would admit to having done it, as a joke. Besides, none of them were in the backstage area where it rolled from, when it came across the stage.

Others, including Burt Drexler, a former Iowa State speech professor, say that lights in the building go on and off without reason.

Some say that Shattuck's ghost moved to the new Fisher Theater in 1973 or1974. They believe that because of some strange things that have happened there.

One actor heard his name screamed out during a rehearsal. No one there at the time would take the blame.

When Joseph Kowalski, an assistant professor of theater, was looking for the light switches in the dark upper backstage area, a voice suddenly said, "They're over by the door." When he found them and switched them on, no one was up there with him.

At another time, Kowalski was working alone in the costume shop when, according to Ken Uy's article in the Ames Daily Times of Oct. 28, 1993, the items he was using, such as scissors and tape measure, disappeared. After a while, they appeared again—not where he would have left them as he worked, but all gathered together in one spot.

Another time, music came over the loudspeakers when no one had started it. When Brooks Chelsvig, the sound technician, arrived, he and Joe Libby, former house manager, went upstairs to look into it. The music stopped. When they unlocked the sound booth, they found one of Chelsvig's tapes in the tape deck. It had been played halfway through. But no one else was there.

Kerry Bell, the co-house manager, and a friend went to Fisher the night before the opening night of Rumors. Kerry realized it was almost midnight, and her friend was dragging her feet about that, but they wanted to put up a display using the actors' photos. Riding the elevator back downstairs from the upper level, Kerry pushed the emergency stop button as a joke. She thought she might as well scare her friend a little. But as she switched it off again, it kept on going, and it kept going for about ten minutes. When Kerry's friend screamed, the elevator moved back up to second floor and the doors opened. Needless to say, both Kerry and her friend left the building on a fast run.

All of these incidents seem to support the claims that the Shattuck ghost had moved to Fisher.

According to an article by Vicki Shannon in the Iowa State Daily of Oct. 30, 1978, Molly Herrington explained the ghost this way: "She's just letting us know that she's still around. She comes out to tell us she's glad we're still doing theater at ISU, since she's the one who started it all."

Shannon quoted Herrington: "At night, ghosts will come out and re-enact their 'big scene.' Sometimes they put together a whole show." Herrington had also told Shannon that old theater troupes always left a gas lamp burning in the middle of the stage to show ghosts their way.

The Ghost Confessed

R. Aubrey La Foy of West Okoboji wrote a column for the Milford Mail called "Memory Lane." At one time he wrote about legends, myths, spoofs, and ghosts of the lakes area of northwest Iowa.

One story was about a farm located about sixteen miles west of Milford and about a mile north. The farm buildings were in the middle of a field and were surrounded by a grove, making it a somewhat "hidden away" place.

An unusual light had been appearing at that farm. The light was quite bright, something like an automobile headlight, but instead of beaming yellowish it was more red.

Those who saw the strange light didn't understand how it could be there. They said it was more like a ghostly aura or maybe an apparition that suddenly appeared in a corn field near the grove—at night, of course. As they watched, they said it slowly moved to the north toward another farm about a half mile away. There, where neighboring farmers knew the brooder house stood, it stopped moving for just seconds. Then, as suddenly as it had appeared, it disappeared.

Many people from northwest Iowa were intrigued by stories about the strange light, and some were all the more intrigued when the light seemed inexplicable. La Foy wrote, "Every night in the fall of 1932, from twenty to forty cars waited on the road to see the strange light." And even if those would-be viewers missed it, they listened to others who either had seen the "ghost" or knew of someone else who had.

Hoping to find an explanation for the phenomenon, in September of that same year someone got a spiritualist to come to the area and stay overnight at a place where the "ghost" could be seen. And it was seen! That night, the light was very visible and very active. The spiritualist saw it and also "saw" a black-gowned woman somewhere at the scene. One person who heard that version said, "A soul in distress!" But other than a few believers, there were many who openly doubted that there was anything like that involved.

Another attempt was made to settle the question. Two upstanding citizens of the area went walking one night in the cornfield and around the farmhouse. They and a few others thought the strange phenomenon was really quite simple—a light of some kind, carried by an ambulatory human. But they found no proof that night.

Later that month, the mystery was solved when the "ghost" turned himself in. A boy living nearby admitted that he had fixed up a light he could carry about in the cornfield. "First," he said, "I poked holes in a milk can. Then I soaked some cobs in kerosene and put them in the milk can. When I touched a match to those cobs, the glow was more red than yellow. That was the light people saw."

When asked why he did it, he said it was more to entertain the people than himself. He said he didn't expect so many people to be "interested and impressed."

And yet, even after the boy confessed to the trick and the report of the hoax made the papers, solid citizens still drove out on that road at night to see if the ghost would appear. They wanted to see it floating back and forth between farms. Others were afraid. When some who hoped to see it got close to where the light used to appear, their friends called them back, according to La Foy. So they must have been afraid, too.

They say folks don't drive out there any more to see the ghost.

But there are people still living in the area today who say they saw it. Was the spiritualist right about the "woman in black"? Does she still roam about in the cornfields or the grove?

A Ghost in the Tunnel

Carole Parker submitted a story titled "The White Blob" or "Mystery on Tree Road" that she had written for her column in the Anita Tribune several years ago. The story was one her husband, Bill Parker, has told his children and grandchildren many times.

About one night a month, especially during the school year, the pupils, parents and teacher had a get-together in the one-room country school. Bill Parker said the school was about a mile from the farm where he lived, near Anita in Cass County in southwest Iowa.

Those nights, the programs consisted mainly of skits, songs, and recitations by the pupils. Then lunch was served. After lunch, the parents and others who came visited with their neighbors and the teacher while the pupils went outdoors to relax. Sometimes they played games. Sometimes they just sat in the yard and talked. Sometimes they told stories into the late hours.

One of those nights—it was in October of 1935, Bill said—some of the pupils decided to go on home instead of waiting around for their parents. They knew they would have to walk home, but they knew the way well. It was a lonesome country road northwest of Anita. So many big trees grew along it that people in the neighborhood called it "Tree Road." The many trees on both sides formed a natural canopy over the road below. In some spots the foliage was so thick that you couldn't see the stars if you looked up at night. But in some places there were openings where the moon, if it was out, could light up the road just enough "to see shapes and forms," Bill said, "but not much else."

That night, although it was in October, not all the leaves had fallen. Many high, gnarled oak branches would hang onto their dark brown leaves into winter, and the evergreens among them would help make the shadows.

The children who decided to start home were Bill Parker, who was eight at the time, and his sister Glada. They were joined by Raymond and Dorothy who were neighbors to the Parkers. All four had gone back and forth to school on that road many times, but that was in the daytime, of course. And they had ridden down that road at night, but that was always with their parents.

The kids knew the road so well that they "knew where the bumps were," and during summer vacations they knew where to find the cattails to take home for their mothers' dried arrangements. They had hunted wild strawberries along it in early summer. Sometimes they just played or walked there, enjoying the fine, cool dust beneath their bare feet where the trees shaded the road.

But that October night, something was different. Yes, it was night and it was dark. But they were tired of waiting around and they thought it was a neat thing to beat their parents home. They decided to "brave it" along the lonesome stretch of road.

They ran, and they slowed again to a walk. Where the patches of pale moonlight broke through, they raced and danced, catching and dodging their own shadows. When they came to the tunnels made by the leafy canopies of treetops, they all ran ahead as fast as they could, as if someone were chasing them. Anything, to get up ahead where a thin patch of pale light came through.

They had almost reached the culvert and they knew that the end of the stretch was just ahead. They would soon be home.

And that's when it happened. The four had just burst through to the end of one of the "tunnels." There, in the spot of pale moonlight, they saw something very strange. They all stopped still and stared, as if they were for the moment struck dumb. Immobilized. Bill described it so well: "As I remember it, no one even screamed. We all just stood there like zombies and stared in silence with our mouths open and chills rippling up and down our spines."

What gave them such a start? A white, formless blob had appeared just ahead. It wasn't a person or an animal. It had no arms or legs. It hovered back and forth across the road, but above it, sort of floating over it.

After a while, it "let out a muffled wail and vanished into the mist along the roadside and into the culvert."

At that moment, without a bit of discussion or uncertainty, all four kids turned their backs on the blob and ran back to the schoolhouse even faster than they had run through the dark tunnels a few moments earlier.

Breaking in on the adults' conversations, the young people tried to explain what had happened. But they were fairly out of breath and their story came in phrases: a big white blob...by the culvert...no feet...hung over the road in front of us...blocked our way...didn't know what it was...it let out a moan and disappeared into the mist by the culvert.

Finally catching his breath, Bill finished. "We didn't wait for it to come out again. We ran back here as fast as we could."

Well, at least the parents knew now why they were so out of breath. They talked it over. Some thought the children had just been surprised and frightened by the shadows. Others thought it may have been a stray animal from one of the nearby farms, perhaps even one of theirs. And, being farmers and parents and rather practical-thinking folks, they decided that those who had to drive over the culvert on the way home should check it out, in case a calf or one of the sheep had taken shelter there.

Bill still remembers staying secure but apprehensive in the Model A while his father got out and got down on all fours to shine the flashlight into the culvert, first from one end, then from the other. But he found nothing. Then he checked the dust on the road near the culvert, but found no tracks, no dust disturbed ahead of where the kids had stood rooted and watched and then turned and run back. He found nothing at all to substantiate their story. He was tactful, however, when he answered. He said, "Well, whatever you saw, it isn't here anymore."

And although Mr. Parker saw nothing, Bill still insists there was something there that night. He still calls it a white blob. And he still wonders what it was. He realizes that ghosts don't always have feet, and that one didn't. And without feet, how could it leave footprints in the dust?

One thing more—the kids saw "the blob" only that one time, nearly sixty years ago. But it could still be hovering along Tree Road or hiding in that culvert. Those four will never know. They never walked that way again at night.

The Ghost of Brush Creek

In the late 1850s, a schoolhouse had been moved in to Brush Creek. But before the turn of the century, the growth of the settlement necessitated a larger building. A brick, two-story, forty-by-sixty school was built in 1877.

In the 1890s, children of school age were used to walking to school, even for three or four miles from outlying homes. On their way to and from school, the Brush Creek children refused to walk past one particular farm. They would beg rides in the buggies or wagons of passing neighbors rather than walk anywhere near the dense woods surrounding that farm.

When the house and the big barn were built, they were set on the edge of the woods, just as many pioneers' homes were. Brush Creek, running nearby, should have been the place for children to go fishing, but they wouldn't go near it. Brush Creek Canyon provided an ideal place for the young people to search for yellow lady's slippers or jack-in-the-pulpits on lovely spring days, but they didn't.

When the parents heard their children talking about the farm, they asked questions. The children said that the woods were haunted. On being questioned further, the youngsters said they had seen someone moving in the brush between the huge oak trees back a few yards from the roadside fence. When they were asked if they had ever been approached by the person, they said, "No. Never. It's more like he wants to hide from us." Another said, "It's too scary. How do we know he won't bother us sometime?" "Besides," a third said, "my big sister Ella quit working there last month, and Ella knows three other hired girls that quit working for the old man before she did."

"He must be real mean, if no one will stay there to work for him. But how can that pretty girl that married him stay? How can Jennie stand it?"

One of the fathers said, "Maybe it isn't the old man that everyone's afraid of." But he didn't explain, and the children wondered what he meant.

Jennie had married the seventy-five-year-old widower on June 6, 1883. She wept at her own wedding, people said. She hadn't wanted to marry the old man in the first place. Her parents had insisted. Many said that Jennie's parents were thinking of themselves and how they could benefit from his wealth.

Jennie was lovely and she was young. Everyone knew there was a young man her own age who loved her and wanted to marry her. Yet she was forced to marry the old man, so much older than she. He didn't even have children or grandchildren for her to learn to love. Jennie didn't care about the house or the money as much as she cared to be happy with someone who really loved her.

The Brush Creek settlement knew the young man who wanted to marry Jennie, but he disappeared shortly after her marriage. Some thought he had gone to another state to find work. Others guessed he'd met with an accident and been killed. There were plenty of rumors as to what had happened. The rumors surfaced again almost twenty years later when people started to wonder if the shadow in the grove was his ghost or if it was himself come back for real, to be near Jennie.

The hired girls who quit one by one told about something or someone, maybe a ghost, that they thought was hiding in the house. They heard noises at all hours of the night, but they never saw anyone else around except the old man and his young wife. Yet food disappeared regularly from the pantry. And in the back part of the house near the kitchen, the smell of decay came through the walls or floor. The girls were afraid their mistress would think they weren't keeping the kitchen tidy, and it worried them. For that reason and because they were honestly frightened, they left.

On the night of August 3, 1903, two people passing by the farm heard screams. They rushed to the house, where they found Jennie crying hysterically. In one corner of the bedroom they found the old man's corpse, his neck broken by hands that had to be stronger than his wife's.

In the investigation that followed, Jennie was questioned. When she was able to overcome her shock and fear, she said the man that killed her husband was a prowler who first strangled him and then raped her. She gave the impression that she didn't know him and had never seen him before.

Jennie kept to herself for about two years after she had been widowed. Eventually, when she began to go out again, some men in the church noticed she was still an attractive woman. One of the men began to court her and soon asked to marry her. She agreed, and they set a date for their wedding. One evening, he came to visit her. He was shocked to find Jennie's body in the bedroom. Her neck had been broken.

The sheriff of Fayette County was determined this time to find the murderer. He swore in three deputies and they searched the house thoroughly, spending seven hours combing every cranny from the attic to the crawl space under the floors.

There, in the crawl space, they found the remains of a man's body, dressed only in rags. With it they found evidence that he had lived there for many years. The body was identified as that of the young man who had disappeared some twenty years earlier. The sheriff and his men were puzzled. They had found the corpse and the garbage, but they still had a problem. Though this person could have murdered the old man two or three years earlier, how could he have killed Jennie, when he had evidently been dead for over a year? How could he have broken her neck?

Today the children still refuse to walk by the old farm. Though Brush Creek is now a part of Arlington, the farm is still there in the northwest part of town. Its buildings are falling apart and its woods have grown even more dense and frightening. The children and the young ladies are still afraid, though the old man and his unwilling bride are buried and the crawl space under the house is empty. Young lovers in Arlington today never stroll by those woods in the moonlight. They feel threatened, they say. They prefer to walk the other way, through another part of Arlington, as far from the woods and the farm as possible—even if their chosen path could take them through the very cemetery where the three people in the story were each in turn safely and permanently buried.

The details that make this story possible were apparently written up by a Rob Robbins for an area newspaper, in the late 1800s when the incidents took place.

The Ghostly Bell Ringer

The limestone church with spires shooting up into the sky can be seen for a long ways in this northeast Iowa town on the Mississippi River. The bells still ring today, but this story took place over eighty years ago.

The bells were at the top of the tallest spire and Janetta had to climb steep rock steps to even reach the ropes. Her father, dead four months now, had proudly done this special job for his church as had his father before him. Since no sons remained, Janetta was to ring the bells this Sunday.

She had often come here with her father, going to the very top of the steeple, before the bells were rung. Janetta would then peek out at the winding Mississippi. Sometimes fancy steamboats would be going past, so elegant and rich, their paddlewheels slowly scooping water. Or she might see some of her father's friends, fishing for some of the huge river catfish to sell at the market.

She climbed the stairs slowly, wondering if she might see any fancy boats today. Leaning against the rough wall to catch her breath, she heard the bells begin to peal. She ran up the last short flight, jerked open the door, and screamed and screamed! The dark figure ringing the bells was her father. Dressed in his black funerary suit, he was rhythmically pulling the rope as he had many times before. He looked at and through her.

Still screaming, she ran down the steps. She did not stop running or screaming until she reached the old German priest's home. Janetta was so terrified and winded that she could only gasp, "Bells, church...my father." The old priest sent her into the house and went to the church immediately.

Janetta nervously stood by the window, not seeing the cool beauty of the fall day. The same river she had looked forward to examining went unnoticed, although bordered by banks of blazing reds and golds. She was still standing at the window, unseeing, when the priest returned. Turning, she pressed her back to the wall and gripped the limestone sill fiercely.

"Did you see...?"

"Janetta, sit down." He gestured toward a large overstuffed chair. "Your father, he is in purgatory and must have a mass said. He is in between—not Heaven, not Hell. We have a mass this morning at Kirche. He will rest then."

Mass was dedicated to Janetta's father that morning, for reasons only Janetta and the old priest knew. True to the priest's word, her father never reappeared, and Janetta continued to ring the bells for many years.

A Ghostly Coon Hunting Story

Daniel J. Zoll's parents used to operate a small country store a few miles north of Waukon in northeast Iowa. It was called the Hanover store. People would come by in the evenings and sit around and talk and tell stories. One of the favorites was this one about coon hunting. This is how Daniel told it:

My father, Emmet Zoll, who grew up in French Creek Township about seven miles north of Waukon, used to tell this story. The October night was dark, dark, dark. Low hanging, misty clouds obscured the stars and the horizon. From the hilltop you could see little circles of light moving through the trees and brush below. It was the weekly gathering of the Silver Creek raccoon hunting society, finding their way through the Gerkey's bottom land on Silver Creek. Each hunter was carrying a kerosene lantern that gave out a dim circle of yellow light, making progress through the deep grass, brush and trees an adventure, if not a bit hazardous.

The Silver Creek raccoon hunting society was a loosely organized group dedicated to the hunting of the nocturnal masked bandit. Some declared that the group was more interested in finding John Barleycorn than raccoons, although that was vehemently denied by all the members. The members of the group, in the main, all grew up in Hanover and French Creek. Most were farmers, but a few occupied different positions in various parts of the county. The parish priests from Hanover and Lycurgus were honorary members and usually attended. Emmet was one of the charter members of the group.

Hunting was not very good this particular night. The dogs had treed only two 'coons. It was getting on toward midnight and everyone was getting rather damp from the mist. Emmet suggested that he and his brother, Willie, should take a shortcut to the abandoned house at the upper end of the Gerkey farm and get the fire started so there would be a toasty meeting place for the usual social hour.

They took Ol' Blue with them. Ol' Blue was the patriarch of the hounds. He was going on 13 years and had one of the best noses for raccoons around, but couldn't keep up with the other dogs anymore.

When they reached the house, Willie got the firewood and Emmet started the fire in the old fireplace. While Emmet was doing that, he asked Willie to put Ol' Blue upstairs. The old house had been built in the 1880s and, like houses of that time, it had a very steep stairwell with a door at the bottom. Well, Willie helped Ol' Blue up the stairs and he wandered over next to the chimney and plopped down. Willie closed the door at the bottom of the stairwell so Ol' Blue could get some rest.

In about a half hour, the rest of the group dragged in and gathered around the fire to warm up and dry off. The fire by this time was burning brightly, casting flickering shadows around the room. Some of the group were sitting on the floor, and a few had pulled up some chunks of firewood and used them for a seat.

One of the Byrnes men was in charge of the refreshments for the evening. He went outside to his hiding place by a fencepost and came up with two jars of pure gut-warmer. As the men sat around the fire, sipping on the refreshments, the conversation soon got around to ghost stories and haunted houses. In those days, people had strong beliefs about such things. The stories got better and better as the fire burned down and the jars neared emptiness. Each storyteller tried his best to outdo the previous one.

At about this time, Bill Gerkey, whose grandfather had built the abandoned house they were in, asked, "Did you ever hear the story about the ghost who used to haunt this very house?"

Well, no one had, so Bill proceeded to tell the story about his grandfather's hired man who had lived upstairs in the house. He was a weird fellow who wouldn't ever say much, but he was a good worker. Well, a couple of nights before Halloween in the fall of 1886, Bill's grandfather heard the hired man wandering around upstairs. It seems that, all of a sudden, the hired man fell down the stairs. He broke his neck in the fall and died. Bill added that his grandfather and grandmother always used to say that every year, around Halloween, they would hear those same noises of someone walking around upstairs, and then a loud crashing and banging down the stairway would follow.

The fire was dying down. There was a lull in the conversation while the last jar made its final pass around the room. It was then that Ol' Blue woke up and scratched himself a few times, his hind leg making a "thump, thump, thump" on the floor upstairs. Everyone in the room except Emmet and Willie froze. Then Ol' Blue got up, walked across the room, his paws going "click-clunk, click-clunk, click-clunk" across the ceiling just over their heads. Ol' Blue wasn't very good at navigating stairways, especially steep ones, and when he got to this one, he missed the top step and came "thump, bump, bang" down the stairs and with a loud thud, hit the door at the bottom.

There was a big rush to get out of that house. The priest from Lycurgus led the charge, with the priest from Hanover right behind him. How so many people could get through a single doorway so fast in the dark is still a mystery to this day, but somehow they did. Emmet and Willie were splitting their guts with laughter.

The Ghostly Guest

The house is in Hawkeye, a few miles southeast of West Union. The two-story house looks very much like all the other well-kept homes in town. But it is not.

Mr. and Mrs. Smith and their family have lived here for many years. During these years they have conducted a ritual that, while it might appear odd to others, now seems normal to them.

The family bedrooms are all downstairs. Although no one from the family sleeps in the single upstairs bedroom, every morning Mrs. Smith goes up and makes the bed, smoothing the wrinkles from the brown and orange coverlet. Why does she spend time making a bed in an empty room? Maybe because the bedroom isn't as empty as it appears. You see, when Mrs. Smith goes upstairs to make the bed, it has always been slept in. The bed is mussed up—the sheets wrinkled, sometimes slightly damp, and the covers pushed to one side. The dresser and chair are always in the same position. Nothing but the bed has been disturbed.

The Smiths say they do not feel threatened and have never heard noises from the bedroom. They wash the bedclothes each week along with their own and they dust and vacuum the room, though Mrs. Smith says the old oak bed is rarely dusty.

Rumor has it that an old lady, neglected by her family, died in that room many years ago. Her death was a hard and lonely one, with no one to comfort her at the end. So she stays on in the room, with a family that cares more for her now than her own did when she lived. But while the Smiths say they are not afraid, they are always careful to keep the door to the bedroom locked. Just in case.

Gretta

There was nothing unusual about the architecture of the house in Calmar. It was an ordinary smaller home, built in the 1920s, with two rooms up and two down, a basement, and a garage.

What was strange about it was that things were happening there when no one was at home. No one that was supposed to be there, at least. Window shades would roll up and down in the daytime, as if someone followed the sun around to keep the house cool. Windows on the east side were opened in the forenoon, as if to let in fresh air. The neighbors said that by noon, they were always closed again. Yet the door was always locked, too, when Dex, the rightful tenant, came home from work.

Dex wondered about these strange goings-on. There were others, too. Some mornings when he woke up, a woman would be hovering over the bed, looking down at him. When she appeared, she was dressed in black and wore a wide-brimmed black hat decorated with pink roses and a pink ribbon. The roses were like the ones on the sturdy old bush in the back yard. A neighbor told Dex they were Tiffany roses.

Dex began to wonder if the woman who had lived in the house many years before he did was showing her displeasure over being placed in a care center against her will. In life, she had always been especially tidy about herself and her home and yard. She had tended the roses herself as if they were her children. Maybe she had come back now to set things straight.

Dex, the paying tenant, slept in a waterbed he had bought before baffles were built into them. Used to its normal movement, he easily recognized when someone standing at the side of the bed pushed down on the mattress, making a wave that moved him up and down, up and down. He got up once to turn on the light and look around, but no one was there. It kept on happening. It grew worse, the bed's movements stronger.

"The pushing presence made me feel smothered," Dex said. "I felt bound by a force that kept me from moving. Once, the bed lifted up with me in it. All of a sudden, I was looking down at the top of the dresser. I could see every item on that dresser. Not in a mirror. It didn't have a mirror. I could even see what time it was on my pocket watch lying there. It was just past midnight."

Eventually, Dex got disgusted with the situation, the unsettling incidents, and the lack of sleep. "I decided to try coming to terms with Gretta, my nickname for her. I said out loud, 'Now, look here, lady. I'm gonna live here. I'm not moving. If you're gonna live here, too, let's come to some kind of agreement. You come and go as you want, but leave me alone. I live here, too, you know, and I intend to stay and to get a good night's sleep every night.'"

His sudden tirade seemed to tone down Gretta's spirit a bit. The bed still moved some, but not as much. The radio started popping on spontaneously, and gentle footsteps could be heard on the stairs to the second floor. Scratching sounds as of branches moving across upstairs windows were frequent, but there were no trees or windows outside the upper level of the house.

With its simple peaked roof coming right down to the side walls, only the end walls and the dividing wall upstairs boasted much wall space. One day, Dex noticed that the inner wall had developed a brownish stain. He checked, but found no roof leak, nothing that would explain such a spot. Besides, the stain didn't start at the ceiling. It showed up in the lower part of the wall. Dex painted over it. Before long, the stain showed through again. He learned to keep the paint and brush handy. He painted that one bedroom wall seven times, but the ugly brown kept coming through, and it certainly defied explanation.

Dex's wife added to his story. She said that once, before they were married, she was in the house alone. "I had the tape player going," she said. "The tape I was playing had one song about ghosts. When the tape reached that song, it went wild, jumbling the music terribly, like a frenzied person trying to sing. But the rest of the songs had come through just fine."

She added that Gretta's house had pushbutton light switches— not turndogs, not up and down flips, not sideways flip buttons, but round buttons you poked in while the other one above or below it popped out. They clicked when you turned the lights on or off using them. "I could hear one light switch upstairs clicking on and off that same day. I just got out of there in a hurry. I wasn't about to go upstairs alone and check it out."

Dex said, "That was the last strange happening in the house in Calmar. Later, I did move out."

Do ghosts haunt the places they have lived, or do they follow the people they have haunted? This couple hopes the latter is not true. They feel they have had their fill of ghostly presences and forces. They say that so far, in their present home, there have been no problems.

The Haunted House

Edie Barnes, one of the girls in the group, hesitated. She knew the house was haunted. So did Holly Carter, who told this story, but she didn't want her boyfriend to know she was afraid.

With a little coaxing and teasing from the boys, the four finally moved up toward the double front doors. Bud Landt's skeleton key didn't work, but Arnold Smithson went around to the back and somehow managed to unlatch a window and let himself in. When he opened the front door from inside, the others joined him.

In the dark, they found their way into the big parlor. Even with some of the shutters closed, enough light came through the windows to lend an eerie look to the room. The few odd pieces of furniture that remained seemed to be draped with fabric. "Probably sheets," Holly said.

"But then," she went on, "the sheets started to move. In front of us, a ghost shot up out of one heap. It reached toward the high ceiling, then stepped to one side and stood on the floor not five feet away. Edie clung to me. She hadn't wanted to come in the first place.

"Next we heard a weird sound coming from a corner of the room. It started as a low crooning that gradually rose to a high, long screech. During that time, everything came alive. White-draped figures shot out from behind furniture, and we heard someone sneezing and someone else laughing.

"I guess the boys didn't want to lose our friendship entirely and on the spot. They told the 'ghosts' to come out and show themselves. They turned out to be some of the other young people that lived near there and some of the boys who had always played around the 'haunted house' and knew it well. As it turned out, we knew most of the 'ghosts,' too.

"We weren't too happy about the trick they had all planned to play on us, but we realized it was Halloween and that they had taken advantage of an opportune situation. We got into the spirit of the thing a little more then and let them show us how they'd managed it. There wasn't much to it, really. They just got under the furniture covers ahead of time and waited for us to come in. I laugh when I think of it now. How scared we were of that house!"

"That house" is a large brick home in northeast Iowa. In structure, it is much like many other large, older homes. It has tall windows, 12-foot ceilings, front and back stairways, and an attic and basement stairway. It has fourteen rooms, two baths, and two large porches. Sturdy construction has made the home last for almost 120 years. The fact that the walls, both inside and out, are solid brick and twelve inches thick has probably helped it endure.

There used to be a gazebo in the yard. It was used, it is said, for serving lemonade and cakes or cookies to family and guests. At one time, when the residents had a young daughter, the topiary in the yard was unique in that evergreens were trimmed into formal shapes of sofas, chairs, and animals. The fancy outhouse matched the Gothic style of the house.

Some remodeling has been done since 1950 to suit the needs of those who bought and restored it, but the original shutters have been kept and furniture has been purchased to fit in with the style of the home. Though some ornamentation remains on the exterior of the house, much of the heavy gingerbread trim was removed many years ago, to avoid the cost and labor of repairing and repainting. Once that trim was removed, the house lost a large part of its "haunted" look.

But before that happened, the property offered plenty of opportunity for a haunting because of its location, size, and appearance. During the years when the house changed from a carefully kept mansion to a neglected, vacant property, several people still recall not wanting to walk past it on their way to school. Others remember calling it "the haunted house" as they drove by with their parents. How that attitude came about could be a result of the nature of early life there.

The original owner had the house built in 1868–1870. His family owned the property for years. After his death, it stood empty for long periods, especially in winter when his widow chose to live in a hotel rather than heat the large house. The couple had a son and daughter. The son married and moved out for a while, but later lived in the house for a time. The daughter returned to the family home often.

The daughter—let's call her Eleanor—was gone often, leaving the house empty for long periods, as her mother had also done. Whenever and wherever Eleanor was seen, she was easily noticed. She dressed differently from others. Sometimes dressed for riding, she would be seen riding a horse or driving a carriage about the area. One acquaintance remembers her as wearing the first two-tone shoes she ever saw. Another said she had red hair. She definitely was noticed and remembered by others.

Eleanor, according to those who knew her, was frugal, some think to a degree of eccentricity. She had money, but never spent much. She had a good appetite, though, and they say she watched for chances for a meal or extra food without extra cost to her. Sometimes she would offer a nickel or a dime for whatever was left, if anyone in her group ordered too much food. At church coffees, which it is said she attended at many of the churches, she would ask for another piece of cake. Others say she chose to sit at the table where the cream pitcher was still full, and she didn't hesitate to help herself.

Eleanor watched for free rides, too. When some high school

girls she knew went to Mason City to Epworth League Camp, they found her sitting in their car, in front of the Hanford Hotel. She hoped to ride with them, of course, wherever they were going. To get her out again, the girls went into the hotel and had her paged. Then they went out a different door as she went into the hotel, and they beat her out of her free ride.

On another occasion, some girls were going on a boat cruise on Clear Lake. Who called to them and ran to join them but the ever-present Eleanor, who was also at Clear Lake that day!

It could be that Eleanor, deprived of family and boasting few close friends, was there alone so much over so many years that her somewhat eccentric presence is still felt. Perhaps, later on, she came back in spirit to the home that was hers for many years. Perhaps, unseen and unheard, she inhabits the attic or the basement or passes unnoticed down the beautiful front staircase and out to the lawn, though it no longer offers her a sofa or a chair or a friendly animal shape.

Now the house is occupied by another family, unrelated to the original owners. Maybe future generations of their family will be told about the times when young people played around "the haunted house" and entered it when it was vacant—or was it?

His Image Returns...Often!

When Jane worked at a nursing home in eastern Iowa, something quite unusual happened. She told her friend Diana about it.

Jane said, "One night, when I was at work, I was just sitting looking at the wall because there wasn't anything to do at the moment. It was shortly before eleven, and all the residents had been in bed long ago. It was a pretty quiet time. All of a sudden, a Native American appeared. Not a real live one, but the image of one. Right there on the wall in front of me."

Diana wanted to hear the rest of it, so Jane went on. "I'd heard of it before, but I didn't believe it. Then, when I actually saw it that night, I believed. And I got really scared.

"When the next shift came on, I felt a little foolish when I told a couple of the day staff what I had seen. They said they'd heard of it before, and so had some others that worked there. They said it always happened at night. They kept quiet about it, though, so the residents wouldn't be restless at night because of it."

One employee said, "From time to time, someone—usually staff—will see that same image. It keeps coming back. Always at night. It's a good thing, too. The residents are always in bed early, and most of them are sound asleep when it happens."

Jane asked, "What else do you know about it? And can't something be done to get rid of it? That would be scary to the residents if they ever saw it. It was scary enough to me!"

Jane was told then that a former resident, a Native American, had died there a long time ago and that it was believed to be his image that kept appearing on the wall, even though the wall is frequently painted over. Jane wonders, Is it only the image of the deceased? Or is it his spirit that comes back in a form we can't understand? Does he come back to haunt his former residence? Or does he come to bring peace to all the current residents and staff?

Out loud she said, "I wish I knew the answers!"

Hollow Haunts

There are several stories about frightening experiences taking place in one of the hollows in Allamakee County. Because of the topography of northeast Iowa, there are many ravines or hollows with creeks or rivers such as the Turkey River, the Yellow River, the Volga, or the Upper Iowa. The deep ravines are the result of water running down and through them for so long that it has worn the limestone away.

The depressions called hollows are usually surrounded on three sides by slopes or limestone bluffs varying in height and overgrown with trees and brush. Caves, once accessible, are hidden by vegetation or have disappeared when their roofs caved in. Because of the numerous creeks and rivers, there are bridges, some in good repair and some closed because they are no longer safe or because they lead to nowhere.

One such bridge is a one-lane span with a dead end beyond it. In fact, vehicles crossing it can only go far enough to park in the grassy area at the other end of the bridge. There is no room to turn around. The terrain is rough with rocks, and it slopes sharply upward. The grass is tall and helps to make it an ideal location for wildlife; it is also fairly quiet, day and night. Bobcats have been seen and heard around the bridge. There is no through traffic, therefore little danger to animals crossing the road.

About sixty years ago, some people lived in a long, narrow shack resembling a railroad car set on a side slope near the bridge. About fifty years ago, the farmer who owned the land built a couple of log cabins and a shed. They are gone now, though they still appear in many stories.

Perhaps because of its secluded location, strange events have taken place in the hollow marked by the dead-end bridge. The stories told about the hollow sparked curiosity and brought on many hunts for the spook or the bigfoot or whatever was in the hollow.

One of the hunts took place on a fall night, when a group of Decorah High School students piled into two cars and headed east on Highway 9. They were as curious as anyone, and they were determined to find out if what they had heard was true.

After leaving the highway, they traveled downhill on an unmarked road. On one of the many turns, three raccoons scampered off the shoulder of the road. Only a few distant farm lights glimmered through the trees before even they were cut off by the bluffs on that quiet, overcast night. No stars or moon brightened their view—only their own headlights as one car followed the other around curve after curve.

The students had been told by their friends that the way to set the mood was to tell scary stories along the way. That was what they did. The stories raised questions in their minds. Was there really a bigfoot in northeast Iowa? Did an eccentric hermit live in those hills? Had someone actually seen tracks and other signs left by a mutated human? Was the notorious wheat-colored creature a pony with a star on its head, or was it a strange monster? Was it the buckskin horse one farmer had reported?

The two cars finally rounded the last curve. The approach to the bridge and the shoulders of the road were soft from heavy fall rains. With the river below and the still, humid air all around, the ground would dry slowly in the gully. Arriving first, the Camaro crossed the bridge and parked in the grassy area just beyond. It would have to back across the bridge to get onto the road again. The Firebird followed, but instead of crossing the bridge, it backed off into a muddy place.

Pete Brandt saw that he had gone too far and had one wheel stuck in the mud. While the other students climbed out of the Camaro, Pete and his passengers worked on getting unstuck. He tried gunning the engine, and some passengers tried pushing to inch the car back and forth, shouting instructions to the others trying to get in or out of the car or the mud. In the general clamor and confusion, none of them paid attention to what their friends in the other car were doing.

Meanwhile, Steve Bryant had talked his carload into getting out of his Camaro. They stood in the grass close to the car and looked around and listened, hoping to settle the big question once and for all. They only heard the river flowing over rocks.

Sherri Jacobs and Tina Miller moved out a few yards toward the nearest bluff. Just ahead, something floated through the brush against the wall of rock. They heard the rustling of wet leaves and grass and the cracking of twigs. A shadowy, wheat-colored figure floated through the bushes and disappeared into a dark spot beyond the old, broken-down cabins. In a lull in the noises from their friends, others near the Camaro heard a loud bawling, bleating sound. Or was it a terrible screaming cry? With the engine of the Firebird still running and the noise of the river, it was hard to tell. Besides, it echoed. No one waited to find out what it was. Screaming, the students piled into the Camaro in just seconds, and it began to back onto the bridge. But the other car still blocked its access to the road.

Hearing screaming and car doors slamming, the others knew something had scared their friends. Six of them promptly lifted the Firebird and its driver out of the mud and onto the firm stretch of road even as they jumped in. They headed away from the bridge, back toward the friendly raccoons and the solid, logical highway before the other car reached the road. Then the Camaro backed off the bridge so fast that it, too, was on the way back to town within seconds.

But that wasn't the end of it. They told their friends, of course, and another attempt to solve the mystery of the spook took place a few nights later when three fellows decided to find the spook or whatever was out there. They planned to go by daylight. They left Decorah after school, but by the time they rounded all the curves and arrived at the old bridge, it was dusk after all. They drove onto the bridge, knowing they would have to back off later. They sat in their car, listening through open windows. When they heard a long, bellowing sound, they dared each other to get out and look into the riverbed below. With the flashlight, they saw a fuzzy, furry thing with a shaggy, flowing mane. It scared them into a mad scramble back into their car. Something below the bridge knocked hard against the metal supports, vibrating the whole bridge and their car with it.

When they backed off and turned the headlights on, they saw something disappearing into a cave-like opening in the bluff, behind a broken-down shack. Feeling relatively safe then, the three decided to get out again and shine their flashlights down into the riverbed. There in the thick mud around the bridge supports, they could just make out the outlines of deep tracks that resembled the shape of a human foot, but were three times as big. The boys left quickly.

Others have tried to look farther into the area of the cave, hoping to find its opening and the creature that supposedly lives in it. They never got closer than a couple hundred feet before they, too, were frightened away by a low, bawling sound or a shrill, screaming, cat-like cry or a shadowy movement against the bluff.

The old buildings deteriorated and were burned down with the landowner's consent. The bridge was closed, due to the weakening of the approach. Only the mystery of the haunt of the hollow remains.

"Is That You, Fred?"

Matt's family had moved to town late in 1991. Matt and Kimberly became schoolmates and their families were soon friends. One night, both families were seated around the table in Matt's home in their town in Cedar County. The hour was late, but they were involved in their game of Trivial Pursuit and weren't ready to give it up.

Suddenly everyone heard the front door open. They weren't expecting anyone at that time of night. Knowing that the house used to be a funeral home, they all thought of the possibility of ghosts. Someone made a comment something like, "I wonder whose ghost is coming back to finish the game with us." Everyone laughed about that. Then one of the group asked, "Is that you, Fred?" At that, the door swung shut again.

One of the players said, somewhat sarcastically, "Gee, Fred, don't go away mad." The door opened again, about halfway, then slammed shut.

No one was laughing anymore. They all sat as if riveted to their chairs and looked wide-eyed at each other and at the door.

The game was forgotten while Inis, Kimberly's mother, asked Matt's mother, "Is this the first time anything like this has happened?"

Sherri said, "I have no idea what went on here before we moved in. But there have been some weird things going on since we came."

Inis asked, "What kinds of things? People you can't see walking in and out and slamming the door, like tonight?"

"No, not that," Sherri answered. "But we have heard footsteps in the upstairs when no one is up there. Sometimes it's in the daytime, sometimes at night."

By then the children were getting curious about what they were hearing from their mothers. Matt said, "Tell them about the chair, Mom."

Sherri told about the old rocking chair in the attic. She said, "Sometimes when we go up there, we find it rocking all by itself."

Matt and Kim wanted to go up to the attic right away to see if it was rocking right then, but Inis thought they should wait until another time. She picked up her things as she said, "Come on, kids. It's time we went home. There is school tomorrow, you know. And besides, I don't want you having nightmares about ghosts."

From that night on, both families referred to the mysterious, unseen caller as "Fred, the ghost that lives upstairs," and Kim's family would add, "in Matt's house."

On another night a couple of weeks later, Kim and Matt did go upstairs in Matt's house. The chair wasn't rocking when they got up there, but that wasn't their main objective anyway. They wanted to see if they could contact Fred. They knew how to use a Ouija board, and they hoped they could get Fred to talk to them.

It took a while, but finally on the first contact, Fred asked for a glass of water. The kids went down to the kitchen for a tall glass of ice cubes and filled it with drinking water from the cold water tap. Back upstairs, they set it on the card table and watched it, but Fred didn't drink it.

Matt and Kimberly went downstairs for a while. When they came back up, the glass was still full. They sat back down to the Ouija board. Matt asked, "Fred, if we count to three, will you drink the water we brought you?"

The pointer moved toward the "Yes."

Matt and Kim started counting. "One...two..." and before the count of three, the ice rolled around in the glass. The kids couldn't understand how it could move, because there were so many ice cubes that they pushed against each other and the glass. Unless—was it Fred?

They both screamed and ran downstairs. But when they came up again, some of the water was gone. They felt that they really were in contact with Fred and they asked him more questions.

"Fred, tell us how you died. Was it a car accident?"

The pointer moved over to the "No."

"Were you sick?"

"No."

"Did you die in a plane crash?"

"Yes."

"Can you communicate with animals, Fred? If you can, make Matt's hamster run his wheel."

The two watched the cage closely, and before a minute had passed, Hampi was running his wheel.

More screams, and another race down the stairs.

When they got their nerve up to go back upstairs, Matt and Kimberly noticed right away that the glass was in a different place.

"Now, how did that get moved?"

Kim answered, "I don't know for sure, but do you think Fred moved it?"

The two decided to stay up there and play Nintendo for a while and maybe keep their eye on that glass, too. Matt wasn't having his usual success. Perhaps his mind wasn't on Nintendo. For whatever reason, he got mad and threw his controller on the floor. Hoping the set still worked, they both looked up and saw the image of a person, from the waist up, appear on the screen before it went dark.

When they ran downstairs again, they stayed there. They haven't tried to talk to Fred since, but they wish they knew more about him and his real-life experiences, before he spent time in the funeral home and decided to make the upstairs in Matt's house his ghost haunt.

The Jordan House Spirit

West Des Moines, Iowa, is home to the Jordan House. The Jordan House was built in different phases between 1850 and 1870 by James Cunningham Jordan, an early pioneer. Jordan first raised cattle and then entered the fields of real estate and railroad development. He also served in the Iowa House of Representatives and Iowa State Senate. While in the legislature, Jordan promoted the change of the state capital from Iowa City to Des Moines. Despite his fame in these capacities, he would most likely have considered his role as a "chief conductor" on the Underground Railroad as his greatest accomplishment. Originally from Virginia, he detested slavery.

A dedicated abolitionist, Jordan helped many slaves on their quest for freedom. His house and farmstead were safe havens for escaped slaves on their journey. Since punishment was severe for harboring runaway slaves, this was a dangerous occupation. John Brown and his party of twelve escaped slaves stayed at Jordan's farm in February of 1859 on their way from Kansas to the raid at Harper's Ferry. The Jordan House is one of several sites in the nation listed as an official stop on the Network for Freedom.

James Jordan and his wife Melinda were the first occupants in the house. After Melinda passed away, James married Cynthia Adams and the couple eventually had eleven children. One of these children, Eda, is said to haunt the Jordan House.

The Civil War was making enemies of the north and south when Eda turned three years old. Eda was a lively, bright child, full of mischief. She might be found playing hide-and-seek in one of the rooms in the Victorian home or jumping out from behind a door to scare her sisters. One day she decided to slide down the walnut banister in the front hall. Since she knew this was forbidden, she waited until the hallway was empty. A small child, she struggled to get to the top of the banister, glancing around to make sure no one saw her. She finally managed to get on the banister and looked down. She hesitated—it seemed much further now than when she was on the stairs. But being a bold child, she decided just to let go and slide down.

Her mother heard a crash and rushed to the front hall. Eda lay at the bottom of the stairs, ominously still. The doctor said she had broken her neck and there was nothing he could do. Eda died within a few days, having never regained consciousness. From that time on, family members would talk about Eda's spirit. If winter gloves were put down on a hallway table and later could not be found, they would say, "Eda's borrowed my gloves. Her hands must be cold." After electricity came, if the lights went out, they would say, "Eda doesn't like those lights. We'd better get out the candles she favors." If an event could not be explained rationally, Eda was the one responsible. They were not afraid of Eda's spirit; in fact, it provided them with some comfort to know she was still around. Perhaps Eda still stays in this house, loved as a child and accepted as a spirit in a home known for its hospitality and generosity to those in need.

Larsen's Poor Gertrude

Larsen Hall, built in 1907, is one of the oldest buildings at Luther College in Decorah. Only Sunnyside, Campus House, and Sperati House are older. Larsen was strictly a men's dormitory for at least thirty years before coeducation arrived at Luther.

Those are duly recorded facts of history, hardly ripe material for a ghost story except for the attraction that old buildings have for ghosts. And there seems to be a ghost in Larsen Hall. She is called Gertrude. No one knows for sure when Gertrude first took up residence in Larsen, but she has been there for many years. Understanding her presence in a men's dorm in its early years depends on what facet of her spirit one accepts. But no matter which Gertrude prevails, her activity is limited to the third floor, in the north end of the east wing and in "short corridor." That's what students call the section between the east and west corridors, at the base of the U. That part of the dorm provides rooms for regular students—men or women, as needed and designated, from fall to spring. In summer, a special program called Upward Bound occupies it for its six-week session. Those students have also learned to share their space with Gertrude.

Parts of the building not used for student rooms provide space for faculty offices and the college health service. Those who work there are sometimes startled by banging radiators or rattling windows on cold, windy days and nights. Those are normal sounds in an old building. Others are not. Babs Goswell, a retired health service director, remembers hearing office doors slamming in the building while she worked the night shift. A nurse, Marny Esbe, says she sometimes hears heels clicking down the hall very late at night, when the other offices are closed.

Most of the stories told about Gertrude happened in the last twenty years or so. Maybe the earlier stories have simply been forgotten. More recent Luther students and staff members, however, can easily recall at least one incident credited to Gertrude, even though they have never seen her. Gertrude has never been known to show herself face to face to anyone. She does take the blame, though, for many acts, such as setting off the fire alarm once or twice a week in the middle of the night. An impartial person could almost feel sorry for Gertrude because she has been the scapegoat for a long time.

B. J. Jones tells about the hot, humid day in late June when she was especially tired after a heavy afternoon class schedule. She trudged wearily back to her room. All she wanted was to flop on her bed for an hour before she had to work a night shift at the Union.

B. J. pushed her door open and let her backpack slide to the floor. When she put her glasses on the dresser, she saw that its drawers were open and the closet door was closed—just the opposite of the way she left them at noon.

The next day, B. J. told her roommate, "I was just too tired to look in the closet. The last thing I thought of before I dropped off to sleep was that maybe Gertrude was in there. By the way, was she?"

Later that same week Jake Fortney, the building custodian, found mud and sand on the floor of the shower in the basement bathroom. The window into the room from outside was also open. Jake had heard about Gertrude and he knew she lived up on third floor, but he began to wonder if she had a friend on the outside who had visited his basement.

Another incident was told by Merilee Stovall and Jane Peoples, roommates their sophomore year. When they settled into Larsen on Labor Day weekend, Merilee chose the top bunk. "It's harder to make up," she admitted to Jane, "but I like the feeling of being on top of things when I get up."

"Not a bad idea for a college sophomore," Jane said.

The feeling didn't last long, though, for Merilee. She had to stand on a chair every morning to make her bed. Then she would do her hair and gather her books and papers for the day's classes and leave her room tidy the way she liked it. She invariably found her bed unmade when she came back in the afternoon. The covers weren't just pulled back. The sheets were tied in fat knots and the blanket was rolled up kitty-cornered and draped over the end of the bed. Naturally, she felt a little perturbed about it and, eyeing Jane directly, asked more than once, "Gertrude again? Why does she always have to pick on me?"

One night Merilee had Jane's stereo on while she typed a term paper for religion class. Tired, and making too many mistakes, she turned the stereo off and went to bed early (early being maybe by midnight). She knew Jane wouldn't be back to their room until a local pub closed.

Merilee fell asleep easily, but was awakened not long after by strains of the song "All At Once" from the same album she'd been playing that evening. She hung over the side of her bunk to see if Jane was asleep. The security light in the parking lot shone in just enough for her to see that no one was in Jane's bunk. Merilee nearly exploded when she realized that Gertrude had visited again and that she would have to get up and turn the stereo off herself. "Everyone says, 'Poor Gertrude.' Why not, 'Poor Merilee?'" she grumbled.

Another time Gertrude visited the room occupied by Rick Workman and Joe Carter of the Upward Bound staff. They had stayed at the dorm over a Fourth of July weekend. The students and the rest of the staff were gone. Returning to the room alone late that sultry

Saturday night, Rick sensed that someone was in the room. He knew it wasn't Joe. Joe had made a spur-of-the-moment decision to join a group on a canoeing and camping outing on the Upper Iowa. Rick had driven them and their canoes to Bluffton himself that morning. Rick was to meet him at the Knudson Canoe rental site across from Will Baker Park and bring him back to campus the next day.

Then who is in here, Rick wondered. He had checked the outside doors a half hour earlier to make sure no one had propped them open. That usually happened when the students were around, so he thought checking them once was enough for that night. He reached for the light switch. The bulb flashed and burned out just as it came on. He tried the fluorescent study lamp on the desk, but both cool-white tubes were gone. Joe had the flashlight, so as a last resort, he lit a stub of a candle left from a murder game they had staged for entertainment the previous weekend. The flame flickered, then burned blue.

When he looked around, Rick saw all his clothes piled on the overstuffed chair near the desk. In the closet, at least a dozen hangers were neatly lined up in a row, with the hooks all hugging the rod in the same direction and each one hung with a long skirt, a dainty summer blouse, a knit shawl, or a braid-trimmed cloak. "And if she wore jeans," Rick muttered, "I'll bet I'd find them in my drawer!"

That night, a heavy downpour during a thunderstorm broke up the camping group just before dawn. When Joe, soaked and muddy and tired, came back up to short corridor, he found Rick curled up sound asleep on the hall floor, still holding the key to their room in one hand and a stub of a candle in the other. The door was closed. In fact, it was locked. And when Joe tried to unlock it, his key refused to turn in the lock. "Gertrude!" he almost shouted.

Only two believable explanations have been offered for Gertrude. Each one attempts to make clear how she came to live in Larsen Hall and each leaves a little to the imagination. One story is that she was a brilliant 1918 Decorah High School graduate who dearly wanted a college education before Luther became coeducational. She was also needed at home to look after her mother, who had been widowed early in World War I and who suffered from a broken hip. Attending a local college was her only possible recourse. She was refused at Luther; the college wasn't ready for female students. Before the year came along when she could have been admitted, she was struck down while riding a bicycle on West Broadway. Her injuries were fatal. Those who believe in that view of Gertrude picture her as a sad but lovely young woman often wearing a long white dress with lace trim and carrying a white umbrella while she hung around for years, waiting to be admitted through the usual channels. She is still waiting. With so much time on her hands, she is likely to do her share of mischief.

The other more grim view is that Gertrude's lover was a senior who grew despondent over the second World War and his plight as a student. With grades so low that his graduation from Luther was seriously threatened, he supposedly hung himself in 1945 in an old ice shed on the west side of Decorah. They say that when Gertrude heard what he had done, she dressed herself in a dismal charcoal gray wrapper and a strikingly contrasting fancy bonnet and appeared at his funeral. Within a few months she, too, died of an unknown cause. Perhaps she willed herself to die. Later, as a ghost, she went up to his former room in short corridor on the third floor of Larsen Hall to look for her lover. Her spirit felt most at home there and stayed from then on, to be as near as she could to his tragic spirit.

The Lost Books of Moses

Some German immigrants believed faithfully that there were two lost books of Moses: the sixth and seventh books. Supposedly these books were used to cast spells on people. The spells could make your livestock sick, keep your cows from milking, prevent your butter from churning, or cause your crops to wither in the field. Often, German-language newspapers available in America would contain stories in serial form that featured the lost books.

One true story from Iowa centered around these books. A German had come from the old country and settled in Clayton County in northern Iowa. He married a neighbor girl and they had three children. She died in childbirth and he remarried shortly. Five more children were born before the second wife died of influenza. Finally, the man married for a third time to Helga, a vain young woman, who was not very popular with her stepchildren. The oldest daughter, Rosa, was nearly the same age as Helga. The new wife and her husband had two children, making a total of ten children in the household.

After ten years of marriage, the farmer died quite suddenly. Rosa, who had been close to her father, grieved greatly. Although her brother and sister had married and moved away, Rosa still lived at home. Housecleaning had always been Rosa's responsibility, as well as a number of outside chores.

Helga inherited everything. Her first step was to inform Rosa that she would have to move out. Relatives of the second wife were contacted to take the younger five stepchildren. The three oldest children were bitter, especially Rosa. Helga would not even let them take their mother's beautiful hand-worked tablecloth.

The widow and her two children now lived in style as the old farmer had been frugal and hard working. The farm was paid for, and there was gold and silver hidden in the old dry well.

Meanwhile, Rosa, who had moved in with her brother, went to her father's friends in an attempt to obtain a copy of the sixth and seventh books of Moses. Most talked about the books but none could produce them. At last, she found the books with an elderly cousin. Rosa planned to curse Helga and her children, by somehow invoking the books. But Rosa's brother, much as he hated Helga, would not allow a copy of the lost books in his house. Nor would her sister. So Rosa had another idea.

A clear summer day was fading into twilight. Helga was baking bread, humming a German tune when she heard thumping noises in the root cellar. Opening the trapdoor, she yelled down, "Stop making that noise, children! I must get this bread baked."

No one answered. Peering down into the dark, damp cellar she could see nothing, but the thumping noises got louder. Dropping the trapdoor, she went to get a candle. Just then her children came in. "Ma, who is that in the ditch?" they asked.

Looking out the front door to the road, Helga could just make out a small figure in a white dress walking up and down the ditch, carrying an open book. Helga felt a wave of panic. "Could you hear what she was saying?" she asked. They shrugged. "Funny words, they must be in her book."

Meanwhile the noises in the cellar were getting louder.

"Ma, what is that?"

"Nothing. Maybe a shelf has come loose. Go to bed."

After the children were upstairs, she yelled from the door, "Go away, you and your evil book!" The white figure never looked up and Helga, too, went upstairs to escape the walker and the noises in the root cellar.

The next evening it started over. After a week, Helga sent the frightened children to stay with her parents, but she refused to leave. The noises and the slender pale figure kept on, night after night, in rain and fog and wind. Although Helga told everyone in the area, no one but she and her children ever saw the apparition. Slowly, her corn crops started to turn from bright green to yellow. This the farmers could see. Much whispering renewed about "those books."

Until now Helga had been considered a desirable match for eligible farmers in the area. She was still young and pretty—and rich. Bachelors had started casually dropping by, discussing the weather or crops. Now that stopped. Despair took hold of Helga. Other than her father, she could not get anyone to come and help with chores or feed her hogs. Even her father was reluctant. He noticed the changes in the crops and noted that the hogs were lethargic, eating very little, and gaining no weight.

Helga's dream of herself as the rich wife of one of the handsome bachelors was disintegrating. She decided she would beg the white vision for mercy. From a safe distance, she threw herself on the ground and pleaded. The pale figure paused, hovered briefly, but then kept walking and chanting strange words Helga couldn't understand. Helga didn't get close enough to see the face of the apparition. Images were now created in her mind of a bleak and lonely future, an old, bent woman living in the poorhouse. Helga turned in desperation to the parish priest. He had offered his help earlier but she had turned him down.

Helga's father and the parish priest met her at the farm in the daytime. The priest was shocked. Instead of the pretty widow who prided herself on her looks, he saw a haggard woman with blue-black shadows under her eyes, wearing a filthy apron. Propped beside the door was an old shotgun.

"I cannot take this anymore! I will shoot her, and I will shoot whatever is making noises in the root cellar," she cried.

The parish priest examined the house and looked down into the gloomy darkness of the cellar. Then he walked out to the ditch, where the green grass grew thick and high, despite Helga's claim that something had walked here for a month or more. No other part of the farm had such lush, green grass. Thoughtfully, he went back in the house.

"Shall I shoot now?" Helga implored.

The priest shook his head. "You can shoot the thing in the ditch or you can shoot in the cellar. It will be the same."

Helga's father looked at him. "What do you mean?"

Patiently, the priest explained. "The figure in the ditch and the noises in the cellar are the same."

"How can one thing be in two places?"

"I do not know how. But it is."

Helga interrupted. "What can I do? I cannot live like this."

The priest was quiet for a long time. "You did a great wrong to your stepchildren. You must change that. I will talk to them. With their help I can remove this curse."

"But this farm is mine. It was left to me!" protested Helga.

"The curse is already at work," the priest reminded her. "Do you want the noises to continue? Do you want these evil spells on you and your children?"

"No, no," she cried. "Do what you must!"

The priest summoned Rosa to church, a place she had not been since her father died. No one knows what Rosa and the priest talked about, but people said Rosa came in with a bulky package and left empty handed. The noises in the cellar stopped. The crops turned green again and the hogs grew. All the children from the first two marriages received an equal settlement.

Helga used her remaining gold to buy another farm on the other side of town. Rosa would take no gold, so Helga turned over the home farm to her. Rosa never married. Today the farm is owned by the descendants of her nieces and nephews. In a place of honor sits the old oak family table, covered with a fine, handmade tablecloth.

A Loud Knock

A retired teacher recalled an incident that took place over sixty years ago at a rural school in Allamakee County. She will be called Maria Thomasin in this story. Maria remembers the details well because she had come in the fall of 1922 to teach in the same school where another teacher who will be called Bertha Atkins had been murdered in 1921.

The date of the 1921 incident is recorded as December 21. Two students had stayed after school that day to erase the blackboards and talk with their teacher, whom they adored. The girls were on their way home when they turned at the corner to see Bertha going down through the outside door to the basement to bank the fire for the night. It was getting dark, so they parted and walked to their respective homes.

The girls didn't know that a passing farmer had seen someone sitting on the hill behind the school that afternoon. He said later that he thought he recognized the man as one of the group that had stirred things up the previous year, when only cast members were allowed to come in to practice for a play that was to be a fund-raiser. Those not allowed at practice had caused a disturbance, and some of them still held a grudge against the teacher for it.

Accounts of the incident indicate that the man seen on the hill on December 21 must have slipped down to the yard after school that day, after the last students left for home. He followed Bertha Atkins into the basement, where she would have been using the big, awkward scoop shovel to bank ashes over the live coals to hold fire in the stove for morning. She could have turned to see why the door had swung open again behind her. She may have recognized the intruder as one of the group who had been denied entrance the year before. At any rate, a member of his family said that he had come home late that day, but only long enough to change clothes and wash his hands before he left in a hurry. Only by bloodstains on the towel could they have surmised that he was concealing a wound on his hand. Perhaps Bertha, noting his angry expression as she turned around, had reached for the shovel again to defend herself. But he was apparently stronger, and in his burst of anger he was later reported to have beaten her on the head with a heavy piece of stovewood. Then he went out, locking the basement door as he left. After stopping at his own home, he stole a horse from the next farm and a saddle from another as he headed north into Minnesota. It wasn't until May of 1923 that the investigation ended.

The effects of the 1921 murder were long-lasting. When Maria arrived to teach the next fall, she could see that the children had heard details from their parents. She knew they were afraid because of what had happened.

Maria already had two years of teaching experience when she came to the school. She had developed a sense of responsibility and had confidence in her ability to handle her job. She and her new pupils had spent two months getting to know each other and had reached a level of mutual trust and acceptance. The lessons were going well. Maria was used to seeing that the pail was full of fresh water. She had caught on to coaxing the basement stove into heating the room above on these increasingly cold days.

On the afternoon of October 31, 1922, the pupils and their new teacher put their books up on the shelf and their papers and pencils into their desks before Halloween treats were passed out. Then they put on jackets and took popcorn balls and apples out into the crisp air for recess. They had no more than settled back into their desks and bent their heads over their books again before they all heard a loud knock on the door. Maria was at the front of the room, helping two young boys with their arithmetic. She asked Tony Baker, a seventh grade boy sitting close to the door, to see who was there.

Tony opened the door. He said, "No one's here at all." Thinking about how loud the knock was and that evidently someone or something heavy had made the sound, Maria excused herself and went out with Tony to look again. Still no one; nothing. The snow shovel and mop hung on their hooks, and the broom hadn't tipped over in its corner. They looked outside, but saw no one. They looked in the outhouses, but all the students had come in after recess. A quick look into the basement gave no answer. By then, it was almost the end of the afternoon and the children were feeling a little shaken. The scary mood of the coming Halloween night was heightened by the unexplained sound.

The children thought about what had happened to Miss Atkins less than a year earlier. Maria tried her best to calm them before dismissal. She said, "It was probably just a dead branch that fell on the roof of the entry, and with the door shut we just didn't hear it right. You all have fun now, tonight. And be careful."

Nevertheless, the younger ones all stayed close by the side of their older siblings and neighbors as they walked home that day. They talked about mysterious sounds and loud knocks and ghosts. They couldn't forget about it. Fear had entered their hearts with that sudden, loud knock. Jeannie Marshall held onto Irene Godwin's hand while she asked, "Do you think it was Miss Atkins' ghost?" Elvin Young asked Jonathan King, "Do you know where the man is that killed that other teacher? Did they find him yet?" and Jonathan answered, "I heard papa say he's still alive and he's hiding." "Well, then, maybe it was him come back to kill again," Elvin finished.

The spirit of the day the knock was heard hovered like a spell over the children and their schoolhouse. It stayed around until the next May, when the man responsible for their fears was found, tried, and punished by hanging. Many elderly residents of northeast Iowa remember the long search. When the fugitive was finally located and justice was served, the children's fears were finally put to rest.

Mossy Glen Mysteries

Mossy Glen is a beautiful valley fed by three springs, thick with trees, and full of moss-covered stones that gave the valley its name. About four or five miles west of the small town of Littleport and eight miles east of Strawberry Point, Mossy Glen is in Lodomillo Township of Clayton County. But despite its serene appearance now, this valley has experienced mysteries and murders since it was first settled in the late 1840s.

The earliest story about the valley concerns a peddler who came to the area selling his wares. One version of the story says an unknown settler or settlers wanted his goods—wanted them so much they were willing to kill for them. Another is that the peddler was killed for the gold he carried, found during the brief Strawberry Point gold strike in about 1858. Legend has it that the peddler was buried at Mossy Glen. There is a cave there, near a stream, and some think his bones lie deep in the cave.

After the peddler's death, strange sounds were heard in the glen and the valley was unusually cool, even in the hottest Iowa summers. John McDonough wrote a poem entitled "Mossy Glen," and in it he refers to the peddler's death: "But his ghost haunts the Glen seeking vengeance/ And howls in the blackest midnight."

Another unexplained disappearance in the early days of Mossy

Glen was that of a local attorney. His wife had died mysteriously while the family was visiting the area. Rumor was that the husband had arranged for her death. Following his wife's death, the man was plagued by misfortunes, said to be caused by her unhappy spirit.

Early one hazy evening, the attorney was seen driving his buggy out of town and heard to remark he had an appointment at Mossy Glen "to take care of this bad luck." He was never heard from again. Some say his body vanished into one of the many sinkholes that dot the glen.

But the most famous Mossy Glen story is the Shine murder case of 1936. Pearl, an ambitious, red-haired young lady of twenty-seven, married Dan Shine, a reclusive sixty-year-old backwoods farmer. The new Mrs. Shine, formerly the housekeeper, had been married and divorced twice before. Less than a week after the April 30 wedding, Pearl and the hired hand, not yet twenty, filed a new will at the Clayton County Courthouse in Elkader. This new will named Mrs. Shine as the beneficiary and first in line to inherit the eighty-acre Shine farm at Mossy Glen should anything happen to Mr. Shine. Within three days, Mr. Shine's "suicide" was discovered by the Clayton County sheriff and a deputy.

After a thorough investigation, officers determined that Shine had been knocked unconscious and put in the small second-story closet where the body was found. A string had been attached to the shotgun trigger and pulled. He was shot in the head. Medical evidence showed Dan Shine had been killed the same day the new will was filed by Mrs. Shine and the hired hand.

The Shine case received wide coverage in the newspapers. It was also written up in a detective magazine. At one time, ten people were in jail in connection with the murder, but eventually Mrs. Shine was found guilty of first degree murder and the hired hand of second degree murder. In addition, three others, two of them Mrs. Shine's relatives, were found guilty of being accessories.

Following the murder, children would go to the glen and dare each other to stay after dark. Those few who tried came home quickly, terrified. They talked about the strange, darting shadows in those woods Dan Shine knew so well. Today children still taunt each other about being "'fraidy cats" at the glen and the Shine murder case is still talked about. Whether Dan Shine ever got revenge is not known. Mrs. Shine and the hired hand were paroled in 1952 and chose to live far away from northeast Iowa.

How many spirits haunt Mossy Glen? We know of at least three. But how many more are there? According to John McDonough's poem, these spirits reside at "a wild rocky gorge in the woodland/ That is called by the name Mossy Glen."

Mr. Bruce Walked *the* Floors

The Bowkers family had been living in a four-room house that was a little small for them, so Mrs. Bowkers had been keeping her eyes open for one that would give them more room.

One day she (I'll call her Paula) drove by an older house that interested her and was available. She liked the looks of it, and when she saw the inside she liked it even more. It was a well-built two-story house in a city in Linn County.

Before long, all the arrangements had been made. The Bowkers family bought the house that had belonged to a Mr. Bruce, and they moved in as soon as they could. The Bruces had built it, so the Bowkers were the first to live in it after both Mr. and Mrs. Bruce had passed away.

The larger house was sixty or seventy years old. It had an enclosed porch and a large fenced-in yard. Inside, the open stairway and the French doors pleased Paula. They had to pay more than they wanted to, but they didn't mind that so much, since the house suited them so well. You might say, the house grew on her, since after they moved in, Paula loved it even more.

Paula and John Bowkers had a son, Johnny, who had enlisted in the Navy after graduation. While he waited to be called, Johnny worked a split shift at a cafeteria. His mother was used to hearing him come home for a while between his work shifts.

One time, shortly after they moved in, Paula was washing in the basement. She heard footsteps right above her, on the first floor. Thinking Johnny had come home for a few minutes, she went right on with the laundry.

Later, when Paula asked Johnny what he came home for, he said, "I didn't."

Paula wondered if she was hearing noises that weren't even there. She was sure she had heard someone walking around up on the first floor that day. But other times, too, when she was in the basement, she would hear someone walking around up there. Always on first floor.

One day when Paula heard the steps again, she went to the door and called out, "Johnny, is that you up there?"

No one answered. She called out again, but still heard no answer. She went upstairs from the basement and looked around. No one was there. Since their bathroom was on the second floor, Paula called out again, more loudly, but no one answered. She looked out front, but Johnny's car wasn't there, so she was sure it was someone else that had been upstairs. But—who?

It puzzled her. She stood in the middle of the living room and said to herself, What's going on? She never mentioned it to her husband or anyone else, though. She was afraid they might think she was "going off her rocker."

John's work hours varied between three different shifts. One night, he was on the 11 p.m. to 7 a.m. shift. That evening at nine, there was a program on TV called "Our Haunted House on the Hudson" that interested her, perhaps because of the recent unexplainable sounds in her own home. When John got up around ten that night to get ready for work, Paula said, "John, you should have come down a few minutes earlier to see this program." Then she told him about it.

John said, "I can believe those things about ghosts. I think we might have one here."

"What makes you say that now?" Paula asked.

"Well, sometimes in this crazy schedule I'm on, I sit in my recliner in the evenings and doze until it's time to go to work, but I'm usually awake enough to hear the footsteps behind me in the dining room."

Paula realized then that it wasn't just in her imagination that she had heard footsteps almost from the first day they lived there. She told John about it, and she said, "Even when I'm home alone, I'm not frightened. But it always feels as if there's someone else living here with us."

That conversation with John brought the mystery out into the open. Paula asked a few questions and got some answers that helped her understand what was happening. Mrs. Bruce had lived in a nursing home for two years before she died. During that time, Mr. Bruce lived alone in the house.

On the second floor, there were two bedrooms. The open stairway led up about eight steps to the landing and then eight more steps to the second floor. Paula began to think about that landing and wondered if something had happened there, or if there was something else significant about it.

After she had found out more about the Bruces, Paula lay in bed one Saturday morning just dozing. John had to be at work at six, so he left about half past five. When she heard someone coming up the steps, her first thought was that maybe John's shift wasn't going to work that day. Thinking he had come back home, Paula sat up in bed and called out, "John, is that you?" She heard no answer, but the steps kept coming.

Paula called out again, "John?" but still got no answer. She got out of bed and went to the doorway. The footsteps had stopped at the landing. By then, Paula's heart was thumping. She looked down at the stairs, but saw nothing. She thought, What's going on? And she continued to ask herself that question for several days afterward.

Paula had put up with the footsteps for about five years, but unable to figure it out herself, she decided to tell her neighbor Gerry about it. The neighbors had known the Bruces for many years. Gerry said, "Oh, didn't anyone tell you? They found Mr. Bruce dead on the landing. He probably was going upstairs to bed and got as far as that. He'd had a heart attack there, and he died instantly."

Paula said, "We'd heard the steps for as long as three or four years before they stopped. They were steps like any male would make, except when I was in the basement. Then they seemed louder. When he was coming up the stairs the last time we heard the footsteps, they were quite heavy, as though it was an effort for him, and his last.

"Mr. Bruce's ghost had been walking the floors, the first while that we lived there. But now that I understand, he doesn't have to get my attention any more to let me know how lonely he was.

"And I'm glad I wrote it all down shortly after we sold the house. The people who bought it probably will never meet Mr. Bruce's ghost, since it seems he left before we did. And I never heard the footsteps again after that last time. But over the years, I thought about Mr. Bruce a lot. I thought he must have been terribly lonely, living in the house alone those last two years. They never had a family, and he must have walked the floors a lot to pass the time or take care of things."

Night Visitors

Only partially awake, John reached up to brush something from his neck. Whatever it was, it didn't budge. He tried again, somewhat more vigorously, but he was half asleep and it was still there. With a fast, sweeping motion, he made a third attempt. It still refused to leave. Finally, he waved his arms around wildly and, in a shrill voice, ordered it to leave.

The vehemence of his words and actions woke John fully. In the dim light from the hall lamp, though he half expected to find some kind of blood-sucking creature attached to his throat, he could see or feel nothing unusual.

When Helen roused and asked why he was restless, John said, "Why, there was something in here. It flew in at the window and tried to get at my throat. Three times I tried to brush it off. So I finally yelled at it to get away and leave me alone. Didn't you hear me? Then I guess I woke up. It was horrible! I wonder if that was old man Johnson," he mused, naming the previous occupant of the house.

As he told his wife about it, John realized he must have had a bad dream. "Worse than a dream," he said. "It was a nightmare!"

On another night, the couple thought they were hearing footsteps on the stairs to their same second-floor bedroom. No one else was supposed to be in the house. Both heard the footsteps. Each asked the other if he or she had heard anything. Then they both heard the next sound. Another footstep?

Over the brass rods at the foot end of their bed, they could easily see down the hall. Hesitating for only a moment, they summoned enough courage to look. They saw only their own reflections in the wardrobe mirror at the end of the hall.

After these frightening experiences in their first two years in their home, John and Helen had no more strange things happen there. They stayed for thirty-five years in the two-story house on the north slope of a well-known part of Decorah. When this story was written in 1988, they were still living there.

The original owner of the house had built it at the turn of the century. Very few others had lived in it since. The people just previous to John and Helen had occupied it for thirty years, long enough for their own peculiar personalities to linger in one form or another. For a long time, when John thought of that awful dream, he chuckled and said, "Helen, do you suppose that really was the ghost of old man Johnson?"

The Nisse or Hulda?

Some things would happen anyhow, no matter what folks do. That's the way it is. But other things just wouldn't happen unless they were made to happen. In that case, someone is to blame.

Sometimes the blame falls on the nisse. They are the little people living among Norwegians and comparable to leprechauns, the mischievous folk of Irish lore. If you've never met a nisse, you should. In a community such as Decorah, where there are many Norwegians, there are nisse all over the place. Some are real; some are wooden representations of the spirit nisse. You'll see them swinging in the trees or smiling or winking from windows in many homes, even from attic windows.

Because the spirit nisse can do both good and bad things, they are often blamed for what others do. It's as easy to blame a nisse, you see, as it is to blame a ghost. Especially if you're a Norwegian!

Well, sometimes a person just doesn't know who really is at fault, so either a nisse or a ghost can be blamed.

That's what happens at one old farm in Winneshiek County. When bad things happen there to perfectly good people, some folks say, "The nisse did it." Others say, "It had to be Hulda."

Maybe it's both. Maybe they take turns.

Hulda is the ghost who is said to inhabit the house on the old farm. She comes from a long way back. No one would think of turning her out. She probably thinks she belongs there even more than the mortal occupants of the place. She used to live there.

Guests who visit for the first time report a strange feeling while in the house. They say it's as if there is something of the supernatural lurking there. And that's before they've been told about Hulda.

Those who feel at home on the farm have come to accept Hulda, and she usually stays in the background pretty much. If you know about her, you might sort of acknowledge her presence when you're out there and let yourself absorb the feel of the place and fit in. But if someone new shows up and begins to act really, truly at home, as if to take over, something's sure to happen to set him down a spell.

Take, for example, a number of years ago, when a couple of fellows lived in the house for the summer. The younger brother, least acquainted there at the time, proceeded to pour his Saturday night bath water into the old-fashioned four-legged tub in the room at the top of the stairs. Just as he sat down and reached for the soap, he saw out of the corner of his eye a woman dressed in black moving soundlessly through the next room, from doorway to doorway. Needless to say, he cut his bath short and went looking for the woman. His brother told him, "You've probably just met Hulda. There's no one else around."

Hulda has been responsible for family photos being turned face to the wall or disappearing from their frames entirely. It's one of her little tricks. She seems to have it in for certain people. She lets it be known quite openly, yet she also has a streak of kindness in her. For instance, now and then the cats are treated to the milk from a worker's thermos. Unknown, of course, to the worker. While he's in the field or barn or machine shed, the cats move lazily up to the house and lap up the milk that has just been warmed in the chipped blue enameled pan and set on the porch by the back door. The worker finds his thermos mysteriously empty when he stops for his lunch break. As he munches his herring sandwich, he wonders if the milk was "borrowed" to feed the cats, or to keep the nisse amiable.

Though some items of furniture in the house when Hulda's family left have been removed by family members, an old organ was left there. As hard as it is to believe, the organ still works, and whenever the people who own the farm have guests, they encourage any guest so inclined to play it so as to keep it in good condition. Though it might not play in tune for them, with enough people singing no one notices. But when there's no one around but the workers, and they approach the house for any reason at all, they are likely to hear the old organ playing as if it were a player piano. One song after another rolls out, each note in perfect tune. Yet no one is in the house. All the searchers can find is a shadow, or a footprint on the stairs—the same stairs on which mysterious footsteps are often heard from other parts of the house. And sometimes the old rocking chair behind the door into the parlor is still rocking after the searchers leave the house.

Probably the most puzzling and distressing incident of all took place last summer, and true to form, it happened to Buck Wilson, the very newest worker. He stepped into the house just after dark to pick up some keys he'd left there in the afternoon. No one was home at the time, but he knew just where to find them. He didn't need a light. All he had to do was step up to the small table in the middle of the first room and pick them up.

But when he did, he was suddenly plunged downward through the cistern cover in the floor. He fell directly into the cold water below. Now, that bordered on the tragic. There was no ladder in the cistern. None had been needed since the cover was rebuilt, because the table was always right over the spot. But fortunately for Buck, his friend John Skaim had gone out to work that day, too, and was waiting in his van, ready to leave. He'd been watching the sky and recognizing all the signs of an approaching thunderstorm. When he thought about how long he'd been waiting, John got a little impatient with "this new help" and went up to the porch to find out what was happening. He found out. Buck called to him from down in the cistern. John could hardly hear him over the increasing howl of the wind. He thought of Hulda and wondered what she was up to. When he went on in, he saw Buck's predicament and almost laughed. He got a ladder and a light and rescued his friend.

Buck asked John, "Why on earth didn't you tell me you moved that table?"

"What table?"

"The one you told me to always keep over the cistern cover."

"What are you talking about? I sure didn't move it. Did you have a light on?"

"No. I didn't think I needed one. Half the time, the lights go out around here anyway, even when I have 'em turned on! But the table was moved, and I fell into a trap, I guess.... If you didn't move it, I wonder who did?"

On the way down the lane, Buck, still shaking and even more violently now as the truth dawned on him, blurted out, "John, that must have been Hulda!"

John answered him easily even as a great horned owl swooped down and buzzed the van's windshield. "You finally realize I didn't have a thing to do with it. Buck, you were just being initiated into the crew out there. It has happened to all of us, at one time or another. You might have expected either the nisse or the ghost to be watching for you!"

No Magic *in the* Water

There used to be many springs in the lakes area of northwest Iowa, but according to R. Aubrey La Foy of West Okoboji, practically all of them have disappeared.

Reportedly there was one on the west shore of Lake West Okoboji, about two miles south of the northernmost point of the lake. Hattie P. Elston referred to it when she wrote White Men Follow After. She wrote about Mini-do-ka, a spring of magic water. La Foy says that generations of Native Americans went to the spring to be healed of their sickness by the medicine water from the spring.

In his "Memory Lane" writings for the Milford Mail, La Foy quoted Elston when he told that a bottling plant was built in 1912 to bottle the water from the spring. An advertisement in the Iowa Lakes Beacon, published in Spirit Lake, promoted the beverage until about 1933, when the factory quit bottling it.

But the spring was still there, and just as its cool, clear water continued to flow, so also did the many stories relating to it.

One story known among the Native Americans became part of the lore of the settlers around the lakes in the 1850s. It seems that a young woman carried water from the spring back to the tepee where a man lay, delirious with fever, suffering from an infected wound. She hoped the water's magic would bring healing; however, the fever became worse. Weary, but determined, she walked to the spring one more time. It was late on a moonless night, and she never returned. Whatever happened to her, they say it was on the same night her sweetheart gave up his spirit in death.

Afterward, on many dark nights, people saw the wispy figure of the barefoot young woman hovering near the spring, as though she still hoped to bring its magic back to the dying man.

Another story concerns a traveler Elston wrote about. The elderly man, tired from riding his pony to the lakes region from somewhere in eastern Iowa, stopped to rest at the spring. When he bent above the rocky ledge and drank the cool spring water, he felt refreshed to the point of wanting to ride on immediately. But first he led his thirsty pony toward the pond that the flowing water had formed below its mouth between the rocks. What the traveler didn't realize was that the pony would get bogged down and trapped in the spongy muck that was like quicksand. There was no one around to help, so the traveler sorrowfully bid his pony farewell and went his way on foot.

For many years, people of the lakes area reported hearing a man's tired voice gently soothing and coaxing, but the only figure they ever reported seeing was that of a very old man in tattered gray clothing. He always stopped at the pool near the spring for a short time and then disappeared, as if his spirit came to try to free his pony from the mud.

Recently someone draining the land around the spring found the jawbone of a horse buried near the mouth of the spring. By then, the old man's ghost was no longer seen. It was as if he had given up his attempt to extricate his pony from the bog.

"Now, I Believe There Are Ghosts!"

Harry Patten said, "Being wakened by noises in the night was bad enough. But hearing them upstairs when the family was downstairs meant getting up to check. I needed the flashlight, since we didn't have electricity. And sometimes I took the rifle along, too, when I went up there.

"If the noises came from the basement, I checked down there. I never found anything. My wife said that whenever I investigated, the noises stopped.

"That was back in 1938. I had taken a job running routes picking up eggs from farmers for a co-op in Malcolm, Iowa. My wife and I and our three boys—they were ten, eight, and four then—had moved into a farm house about three miles south of Brooklyn, in Poweshiek County. The house belonged to my uncle.

"It was a two-story, wood-frame house, painted white. It was on the west side of a north-south road. My wife and I and the boys slept in the two downstairs bedrooms. We never used the upstairs.

"So when we heard noises up there, we never knew what was going on. Sometimes it sounded like someone was walking around up there. Sometimes we would hear a thump. The thump always woke us. There were other sounds, too. Sometimes we thought we heard someone talking in low tones. It was more like a muffled mumble than clear talk, and we couldn't understand what was being said.

Usually it was only one side of a conversation that we heard. Then there would be a pause before the talking went on.

"One summer night when we had our windows open, we heard a muffled mumble outside our north bedroom window. Our first thought was that some young lovers were parked out there on the road, out of sight from the house. We tried to ignore it. But then I decided I'd better check.

"I went out to the porch and looked toward the road. No car there. But while I was listening, something else happened to make me really wonder what was going on out there. I noticed that Sabrina, our three-year-old purebred white collie, was sitting on her haunches, near the door, and looking one way, then the other. Then she gave a quick, sharp bark. Not a friendly one at all, as if to greet someone she knew. It was more as if she heard something but didn't know what or who or exactly where.

"That was when I started to believe there were ghosts. If Bri could sense someone or something I couldn't see, I decided there must be a ghost haunting the place.

"One morning when I went to work, I left by the south kitchen door. After I left, my wife heard the sounds of footsteps coming down the stairs and going out the back door—the north kitchen door. I had gotten my own breakfast and left early, so she and the boys were still in bed. When she got up and checked on the sounds, she found the north kitchen door unhooked. We kept it hooked because we used the south door. We wondered for a long time how that north door got unhooked that morning.

"The house had belonged to my uncle, my father's older brother, since before I was old enough to remember. He still lived there until I was in high school. He and my aunt raised four children there. They moved to Brooklyn around 1930. If someone else lived there from then until we moved in, I don't remember who it was.

"When we heard the noises, we wondered if my uncle's family

had ever heard them when they lived there. We finally told my folks about the footsteps and the voices, and they said they knew before we moved in that the house was haunted, but they didn't tell us. They knew, because my aunt had talked about it to them.

"I remember that my aunt had told stories, but I didn't believe in ghosts then so I just forgot the stories. I do remember that she told about seeing a light coming across the field just across the road from the house, when no one was out there carrying one. I think I remembered that story because I couldn't understand how it could happen, but she said it did happen, and often.

"Later, after we talked about it more, my aunt said that one time when they were gone for the evening, some of their neighbors passed the house on their way home from town. They said they saw people dancing in there. When my aunt and uncle got home, though, everything was in order.

"When my uncle's family still lived in that same house near Brooklyn, my cousin came home one night after dark. He went to put his horse in the barn, just like always. He knew the barn well, so he didn't light a lantern or anything. Pretty routinely, he led the horse to its stall. But when he reached into the manger for the halter to put it on the horse, he touched something. It wasn't the halter. Whatever it was surprised him pretty much, because he left the horse loose in its stall, hurried out of the barn, and went to the house real fast and went to bed. He kept thinking that what he had touched in the barn felt more like a person than anything. But he couldn't be sure, because without a light he didn't stick around long enough to see what it was.

"The next morning when he went to the barn in broad daylight, the halter was on the horse.

"Some people say that when a house is haunted, it's because someone died there, maybe even a tragic death. My mother said she heard that a man had been murdered in that house so long ago that people didn't know much about it. She didn't know who he was or when or how it happened.

"I got used to the idea of the ghost. We kept hearing the strange sounds and voices all the while we lived there. Eventually, I stopped letting them disturb me. I would just say, 'That ghost is back again!' and then I'd roll over and go back to sleep.

"Another family moved into the house after we moved out. I always wondered if the next family ever noticed the ghost.

"About two or three years later, a neighbor bought the farm. He tore the house down and built a new one. Then when Interstate 80 went through there, the road was closed a mile south of the farm, so now it's a dead end road. A good place for ghosts, since then."

One Family's Sense of Spirit

There are individuals who have dealt with the phenomenon of strange happenings over a period of years. The resulting effect, or perhaps the cause, is a special sensitivity to spirits or ghosts. That sensitivity somehow becomes an element in the life of the person. It seems that several members of a family may also possess the sensitivity and be affected by it. One family's experiences, as told by the mother, spread over the years from 1954 to the present.

The mother, Colleen, said that when she was about twelve, she had the same scary dream several times, just two or three weeks apart. She always woke up before it was over. At the time, she lived in her parents' home about three-quarters of a mile west of McGregor.

A band of gypsies camping farther west, towards Giard, sometimes came by their house on the way into town. Most people around there had heard of them and had seen them occasionally, as had Colleen and her family.

One of the gypsies appeared in her recurring dream. He'd be slowly walking down the road and around the bend about two houses west, approaching the house where Colleen lived. In each dream, Colleen would see that in one hand he held a knife with a long, shiny blade. She would always wake up then, before he came any nearer.

After several dreams like that, on a very real Saturday afternoon, the phone rang. Colleen's mother answered it. It was a neighbor screaming hysterically, "Lock your doors. A gypsy with a knife just threatened me and he's headed your way."

"Mother told me," Colleen said, "to quick go out on the porch and lock the door. I just stood there frozen. It was an enclosed porch with windows all across the front and sides. My mother went out there, and she had to crawl on her hands and knees beneath eight porch windows. She got there just in time to lock the door before he started rattling it to get in. Then, while he stood there looking in, Mother crouched behind the lower, solid part of the door. She didn't have time to get back in the house.

"Finally, when I saw her predicament, I could move. My sisters and I knew we had to help her to protect our family. We ran and locked the other doors before he got to them. He tried each one. He didn't get in, though. And after that real experience, I never had that same dream again.

"But other things started happening to me, and I wondered if the dreams had awakened a special awareness in me of the unusual.

"By 1967 I had married and we had started our own family. We lived in a three-bedroom house in a town in Winneshiek County. Amy was our youngest at the time. She was about three and had a bedroom all to herself, across from ours. No one else in the family noticed anything unusual, but I could hardly breathe in her bedroom, near the closet. I could feel a presence there, and it was cold.

"Trying to get rid of the feeling, I painted Amy's closet and papered her room in happy colors. It made no difference. During the night, she often woke up crying. I would jump up and go to her room, but I could never go past her doorway. Something always stopped me. I would call, then, for her to come to me, and she would.

"One very early morning, I woke up hearing a child crying outside. I jumped up and ran downstairs within two seconds. I unlocked the door and went out to Amy, who stood there facing the house and crying. She was too short to reach the lock, so I can't explain how she got outside when the door was locked. It was really weird!

"At that time, our good friends had a hypnotist staying with them. Because of my reactions to strange phenomena, I had also met him. One evening, under hypnosis, he asked me to try to communicate with the ghost in our house. Out of that experience, the following explanation came to me.

"The ghost was a woman who had died, leaving her older sister all alone. She had stayed in the house, as a ghost, to protect her sister. When the older sister moved out, the spirit stayed around and spread her mantle of protection over Amy.

"The hypnotist suggested that I confront our ghost. I did. Still under hypnosis, I thanked her. I said to her, 'Your sister has moved away, and so she doesn't need you here anymore. She has found peace wherever she is. As for our family, we're all O.K. and we don't need your protection. Please leave us alone and go and find your peace, too.' The next day brought a great change in the atmosphere in that house. It was as if someone had opened a window and let the fresh air in. The ghost was gone. After that, Amy never again woke up crying during the night."

Then Colleen went on to another incident. She said, "The next year, my grandfather died. He was in his nineties. He had been healthy to the last and had lived a good life.

"We were all at Monona for the funeral. During the services, I began to wonder if I could communicate with his spirit. I sort of thought-spoke, 'If you can hear me, Grandpa, show me some sign.' Just then, the lamp behind me went out. I never did tell that one to anyone before. It definitely startled me then, but I kind of forgot about it until now.

"Not long after that, things started happening that affected others in the family. In 1973, we moved into an apartment house we owned. We already had a tenant living upstairs, so we moved into the downstairs apartment. There was nothing unusual about the house itself, and I had no bad feelings about the apartments. But out in the back yard, there was another house, a smaller one, with one room up and one down, that we thought we could use for storage. There was already some furniture out there, in the upper room, when we moved into the apartment in the front house. We found an old cot and a rocking chair there. The steps were narrow and steep, so we wondered if someone had moved the furniture up and in through the window and just didn't want to take it down again. Our girls thought the little house would make a good place to play. They took their Barbie dolls and houses out, and it went all right until dark. Then they would run back into the main house. Whenever I went out to see what had scared them, I would feel as if a bad spirit was there. When I listened to my feelings, I thought someone had met with a tragic death in that house.

"I felt that I had to do something about it, if we were going to keep on living in the apartment. I went to the Decorah Public Library and checked out a book on hex signs. I made one then, to hang inside the 'playhouse.' After that, I felt more comfortable about it. But once, the girls wanted to have a slumber party out there. They went to a lot of work to get it ready and take their blankets and pillows and all that out; but as soon as it got dark, they hurried back into the house with us, where they felt safer.

"Before our upstairs apartment tenant moved out, she told me a little about that house in the back. She said that a long, long time ago, a previous landlord had shot himself in it. His spirit must have hung around through the time we lived there. All those years we stayed, I had bad feelings whenever I was in the house in back.

"Strange feelings kept on coming to me, too. I was visiting relatives in St. Louis once. In different rooms in their house, I felt different vibrations. When I stood looking out the front window at the other houses and yards in the block, I sensed that someone had once stood there and watched a person drown. I told my aunt about it, and she said it was true. Before the other houses were built, there was a lake out in front of the house my aunt was living in. A woman no longer in the area had actually stood at that same window once and watched her son's boat capsize on the lake. He drowned before anyone could get help.

"Our family moved again, a little later. We have a spirit living with us now, in our present home. Our oldest daughter, Tina, was the first to see her. She woke up one night and saw a woman standing in the doorway of her bedroom. That was back in about 1979. Tina's married now and lives in another state, but a couple of years ago I woke up one night and saw a woman standing in the same doorway.

"My husband and our other daughter, Debbie, have both heard her footsteps on the stairs at night. On two occasions, Debbie's music box that's been broken for years started playing during the night, and Debbie felt the presence of someone in her room while it was playing. She's eighteen now, and a couple of times lately, Deb woke up screaming, she was so sure someone was in her room other than her family.

"So far, this spirit seems to be harmless, so we haven't confronted her or put up a hex sign. But the more I think about it, the more I wonder how long our family will be having such unusual things happening. Even Amy, after she moved into a new apartment in another state, has heard unexplainable sounds, and strange things have been happening to her TV.

"Life would definitely lack something if this sense of spirit in our family ever came to an end! I just hope that all the spirits that visit us will be harmless, or that if they are hard to live with, we'll be able to confront them or deal with them to everyone's satisfaction."

One House, Many Incidents

When pioneers came to northeast Iowa in the 1850s, many lived with friends, relatives, or whoever was willing to extend hospitality, even if it meant two families living in one small house. Some lived in whatever was available until they could build a home. A few families that had little money left after their passage by sea and by land found shelter in caves in the bluffs. In these, their children were born.

Many were soon able to build small homes. They were often one-room log cabins like the Egge cabin that stands behind Vesterheim, the Norwegian-American Museum on West Water Street in Decorah.

The pioneers' families expanded, however, and larger homes were needed. Eventually, successful crops were produced, more wealth became available, and lumber was hauled in wagons and used for building larger houses.

In rural northeast Iowa, there are still many large homes to remind us of those years. They are old now, some of them 100 to 120 years old, yet some are still used.

One of these shows signs of being haunted. It is a house that looks as if it were made for ghosts—a white frame structure with fourteen rooms and twice as many doors. It's a two-story with basement and attic. On the attic level are several dormers on each side, offering a clear view of the countryside. It seems that no matter who is living in this particular house, strange things happen there. The ghosts make themselves known in various ways and to various inhabitants, but the ghosts stay, and they carry on their "lives" both in and out of the house.

All but the dormers are tall, narrow sash windows. Recent tenants have found these opened and closed by someone else's doing, not their own. The door to the bottom of the back stairway opens and closes by itself, squeaking as it does.

At different times, different people have moved in, but none of them have stayed long. Though the present tenants use only the ground floor, they have heard sounds coming from the upstairs rooms and the attic. Footsteps on the stairs at night are not unusual. They seem to be made by a gentleman wearing boots. At times, the gentleman seems to be very tired, as his footsteps are very slow.

A double line of old, knotted cedars outlines both sides of the path to the front door. Many years ago, they offered protection from the weather for passengers who came in at the stage stop nearby and approached the house for a night's shelter. They lead right up to the doorstep.

One tenant bought a deadbolt for the front door, but found it gone from the kitchen drawer in which he had placed it. No one knows how it came to be in his car later, in a box of totally unrelated items that had never been inside the house.

On a still, humid day, dampness in an old house can make doors stick. Why, then, did one person alone in the house hear doors on the second floor open and close? When they had definitely been closed, they would be found open upon the tenant's return late at night. Or, if they had been left open, they were later found closed.

Having been alerted to the strange happenings, another tenant who made a trip up the wide stairway to the attic in the evening would be sure to turn off the attic lights on his way down. They were on again when he returned in the wee hours of the morning.

A younger tenant enjoyed a cup of coffee in the living room, then placed her cup in the sink. Hours later, when the woman washed the dishes, her cup was not there. Weeks later, after a thorough search, she found it in the room at the top of the stairs.

Another puzzling incident in the same house involved a set of lost car keys. The owner, out of necessity, he thought, had another set made. Imagine his surprise when he found his set hanging on a nail in the top of the closet at the top of the stairs! Even more puzzling, considering that no one could ever get that closet door open until the day the car keys were found up there.

One particularly stormy night, the most startling incident of all took place. The people living in the house at the time experienced more activity than usual that night. First, the owls kept them awake. Then the wind came up. Their banjo clock had just struck one when they heard an upstairs door open and close. That was followed by a thump on the hall floor, then the sounds of someone wearing boots coming down the stairs and bumping a suitcase against the walls. Next they heard the front door open. Then came a new sound. The tenants wondered if there was a prowler in the house. They got up to check the windows. They shut the stair door again, remembering that they had closed it when they went to bed. They looked down the drafty hall toward the front door. It stood partly open. They opened it wider to look out. There, in the dark of the stormy night, they could hear the sound more clearly. With a terrible rush and clatter of horses' hooves, they heard the stagecoach approaching. It pulled up between the rows of cedars in front of the house. During a flash of lightning, they saw the wind whip the branches of the cedars and the flaps on the coach so that they blew out horizontally from their fastenings. The lanterns of the coach were no help at all. They weren't burning.

In the next burst of rain and brilliant lightning, the watchers could see that the restless horses paused at the doorstep only a few seconds, just long enough for a passenger to step up into the coach.

There was no driver—only the black coach, the nervous horses, and the night passenger whose boots disappeared into the coach just before the door panel was closed.

Those who tell about the old house and its ghosts and the mysterious night coach know that the old stage road had been replaced many years earlier by a farmer's field separated from the houseyard by a sturdy fence.

Over *the* Fence *and* Out!

The moon had turned its dark side toward the earth. The only light came from a simple bulb in its sheltered socket on the gatepost, out by the road that led north out of Fairbank.

The cemetery is there, on the north edge of town, partly in Fayette County and partly in Buchanan, as is the town.

With his pant legs rolled up to keep them from being soaked by the late evening dew, Robbie whistled his way along the drive that took him across the cemetery. Although the old, dented bucket was over half full, he carried it easily—he was a nine-year-old who had no cares to weigh him down. Even he knew that ghosts aren't usually found in cemeteries. They're supposed to inhabit the places they used to live in. Here, there were only the very dead.

It was Robbie's responsibility that night to bring home the pail of milk from the family cow over in the pasture on the other side of the cemetery. Mother would have a big pecan roll ready for him to enjoy with the fresh milk. His smile, wide and bright as always, warmed him as he thought of it. That will be a treat, he thought as he looked ahead through the darkening night toward the church.

Robbie finally reached the taller, bulkier tombstones near the southwest entrance. Anticipating the warm glow of light from the parsonage windows just beyond the church, he was startled by two glowing red orbs dead ahead. They dimmed, then brightened as he watched. His first impulse was to reach down to see whose pet was out in the night. As he edged around the last monument and bent to focus on the poor creature, a third red glow pierced the darkness. That is nobody's pet, Rob thought. Not with three eyes! He held tighter to the handle of the pail as he took a step forward only to feel wet, clammy hands reach up from a freshly dug grave to grapple for his ankles.

The dewy moisture helped him tear free. As his arm flew out and up, the milk spilled all over, and Rob literally vaulted over the fence, clearing it easily.

From that day forward, Rob wanted absolutely nothing to do with cemeteries.

Rob died on March 25, 1993, at the age of 64. He was buried in that same cemetery—the Fairbank Cemetery in Fairbank, Iowa.

R.I.P., Bob!

Paddy's Prophecy

One story told by Mr. and Mrs. James Henderson of Clermont involves his father's farm and Paddy Riley, a flamboyant Irishman who was considered a sort of prophet by some of the local folk.

Bert O. Henderson, James's father, bought his farm in 1909 from an Irish family. At the time of this writing, his descendants still lived on this farm in the white, two-story home, five miles northwest of Clermont. James's son and his wife, Bert and Zelpha Henderson, lived there. None of the family had ever seen or felt the presence of ghosts or spirits in the cheerful home. But it was not always so.

In 1931 the postmaster of Clermont, G. H. (Gus) Hackmann, received a letter from a Mr. F.B. Kann of Eatonia, Saskatchewan, Canada. Mr. Kann was interested in information about a haunted house he thought was five or six miles outside Clermont. He, his siblings, and his parents had lived there many years before. Kann told of a rumor that a priest, excommunicated from the church, had been murdered in the northeast, upstairs bedroom.

When Kann's family had first moved into the house, his mother had noticed a large dark stain on the floor of this bedroom and some dark spots on the walls. According to Kann, she had tried a variety of "sure-fire" cleaning products, had scrubbed and varnished—even tried to paint over the spots. But the spots always returned, starting small and gradually growing larger until they were the same size as when she started. His mother became so frightened she refused to go near the bedroom and constantly talked of moving out of the house. Eventually, none of the family would go near the room.

Kann recalled his parents had asked a local Irish priest to help them. Intrigued by this unusual request, Hackmann did a little research and wrote back to Kann.

Hackmann checked with local residents. He did not find anyone able to verify the murders, but he did find that a parish priest had been called in and an exorcism had been performed. After the exorcism was completed, the priest returned to Ireland for a visit.

He also found that Paddy Riley had told the neighbors that if an exorcism were done, the priest who did it would be dead within three months. Paddy lived a mile north of Clermont, at the top of Dibble Hill. Nothing remains there today except a few lilac bushes and a depression in the ground where Paddy started an unsuccessful gold mine. But stories are still told about the fiddle-playing, yarn-spinning Riley and his gift for telling the future. Parishioners told Hackmann the priest did die within the three months, just as Paddy Riley had predicted. A history of the parish shows that a priest died of pneumonia in 1891 while visiting Ireland. Local people said the spirits returned to the house, and weird and spooky incidents were taking place, although no one had a specific example.

Kann agreed with this as he remembered his parents were finally forced by the spirits to move. He did not give any particulars, but life in the house became unbearable for the family. They could no longer live in the house and feel safe. After they moved, the house was rented for some time until Mr. Henderson bought the farm. One renter stayed less than a day. He said the noises from the upstairs bedroom were so loud he could not sleep.

The last letter from Kann is dated May 14, 1931. The family believes that Bert O. Henderson wrote back to Kann and, in a no-nonsense fashion, explained that he had no trouble with ghosts.

There are very few Irish descendants left today. No one asks or knows about the murder, the mysterious death of the priest, or the dark stains that refused to go away.

Paddy Riley, who some say could tell what tomorrow would bring, died long ago. All that remains of him is a pencil sketch done by a Chicago artist. The sketch of Paddy, his fiddle, and his house now hangs in the library of Montauk, former Governor Larrabee's mansion outside Clermont. It is entitled "His World." But that world, and the mysteries of it, have disappeared.

"Please Excuse Us, Augie"

Heidi was a resident assistant (R.A. for short) in Noehren Hall on the University of Northern Iowa campus in Cedar Falls. As R.A., she talked with many of the residents of Noehren as well as other dorms. They came to her with their questions and problems. They also came with stories they heard from friends. The stories and conversations often lasted far into the night.

The stories Heidi heard most often in her last term as R.A. centered around a man who was seen several times walking around in the corridors at Lawther Hall. He definitely wasn't a close friend of any of the current students, according to the girls who told about him. In fact, he hardly seemed to fit into the place and times. The girls asked Heidi if they ought to report this stranger to campus security. Heidi felt a need to find out more about him first.

Heidi had gone over to Lawther one evening earlier that fall, before the hall opened for the semester. She was helping Cindy and Stacey do a large bulletin board to have it ready for opening. As they mulled through a box of letters of all shapes and sizes, looking for the right ones, they saw a man walk by. He was wearing what seemed in one quick glance to be a uniform. The girls knew there shouldn't have been anyone else in the dorm at the time, especially at night—unless he was a repairman or custodian—so, all together, the three followed him. He went up the dark, steep stairs at the end of the hall, where he selected a key from a ring of keys looped in his belt and unlocked the door. He disappeared at that moment. They saw no one in the attic or anywhere near the stairs, and they found the door at the other end of the attic locked.

A bit shaken, they went back to their bulletin board project to finish it. That night they all went over to Heidi's room at Noehren to sleep on mattresses gathered from nearby rooms.

A couple of months later, after classes started and everything was rolling along routinely, Heidi offered to help the Lawther R. A.s again. They had to get ready for a special event held every year at Halloween. It had become a tradition to decorate the Lawther attic for a fun, spooky evening. Students from other dorms were welcome.

This was about the twelfth time the event had been held, according to what the R. A.s were told. Their responsibility was to prepare the attic so that all who came could walk down its long, dark hall, hear a creaky door suddenly slam shut, or hear a click of a lock in the door at the far end of the attic followed by a haunting, drawn-out laugh or a terrified scream. All of it was intended, of course, to give the impression that a ghost or ghosts haunted the attic.

Just before the Halloween event, several residents of Bordeaux house in Lawther laughed about the new arrangement on the bulletin board near the kitchen door. It referred, in part, to the "scary, spooky, bone-chilling night" to be held in the attic. They didn't think their bones would be chilled by it. But an hour later, when they came out of the kitchen, they saw that the letters had been rearranged to read "Augie will return to haunt Bordeaux house."

The girls didn't recognize the name Augie in connection with anyone they knew, and no one else was around at the time. They had no idea who had changed the message.

After that happened, there was more talk about unexplainable incidents and the possibility of real ghosts "living" in the attic or anywhere else in the dorm.

In those late night talk sessions, both at Lawther and at Noehren, other stories came to light. Barb, a Lawther resident, was sleeping in her own room one night. She thought she heard her roommate Krista come in, run the faucets, and climb into her top bunk. During the rest of the night, Barb woke up several more times to the sounds of running water and the creaking of the bunk above hers. In the morning, when she asked Krista why she was up so many times, Krista said, "I wasn't. I stayed over in Noehren with Susan. I just came in while you were in the shower."

Shelley, another Lawther resident, reported seeing a strange "black aura" floating around in her room. She said the shape hovered over her study lamp, moved around a little, and then was gone. She said, "It scared me. I didn't know what it was, and I still don't."

Cindy said she had often felt as if she was being watched by someone other than her roommate or friends, but as R.A. she couldn't let it upset her. She just thought other girls were hanging around, trying to decide whether to bother her with their problems.

Sometimes students heard noises at night, during quiet hours, especially in the time of year when late fall begins to change to nearly winter. Sometimes all was quiet, with many students gone to the library or a concert or play for the evening. When they return, they find pages turned, books moved, notebooks closed. During the night some reported that their covers were sometimes pulled off.

Barb told Heidi about a cold area in front of that bulletin board in Bordeaux house. She thought it was the spot where Augie went in and out of the attic, and maybe still does.

Shelley said, "And that's the exact same spot the weird black aura disappeared, when it left my room!"

Others told of lights being on in the attic when no one was allowed to be up there, or of loud thumps on the ceiling of third floor, or of sounds of furniture being moved above the third floor rooms. There were many nights scary enough to send all the girls from that floor down into rooms on first or second floor for the rest of the night.

After a number of stories came to light, Cindy and Stacey decided to get to the bottom of it. Heidi offered to help. At the Donald O. Rod library, the archivist helped them locate copies of The Northern Iowan from the past few years. They realized that browsing through so many copies would take more time than they had, so they decided to start with some late October issues.

They found there had been similar occurrences over a period of at least ten years. They also learned that the Lawther Hall Halloween event had been held in "Augie's Attic" for several years. The news editors and staff writers spoke openly of "Augie's Attic."

Several stories agreed as to who Augie was: a soldier who died in the attic of Lawther when the building was used as an infirmary during World War I. Since then, the girls concluded, "His ghost now lives in the attic and crawl spaces up there, as well as in other top floors of Lawther!"

During World War I, Augie might have been one of many victims of tuberculosis. On the other hand, maybe Augie wasn't in the infirmary on account of his own illness. An article in The Northern Iowan suggested that he was possibly visiting his girl friend who was sick in the infirmary, took sick himself, and died there in the attic.

However it happened, Augie apparently died there and has lingered in the attic ever since. He has been seen walking the halls, climbing the stairs, unlocking doors, and roaming in and out of rooms on the upper floors of Lawther.

Some residents reported that Augie wore a pin-striped suit when they saw him. Others said he was wearing an old army uniform. So he could have been a soldier, or he could have been a boy friend who dressed up "spiffy" to visit his girl.

Thoughtful, practical Heidi told the girls, "Maybe we'd better ask Augie if he minds if we invade his quarters to decorate his attic and hold this event. I know it's eerie and unexplainable, but all the stories

I've heard lead me to one conclusion: Augie's ghost lives in the attic of Lawther Hall, so it's only right to call it 'Augie's Attic' and to ask Augie to forgive us for disrupting his life."

Porter House Ghosties

Visitors to the red brick Victorian Porter House Museum on West Broadway in Decorah often experience an indescribable feeling as they ascend the lovely stairway to the second floor. They feel a presence of some kind there, its true nature unknown to them. Others, even members of the current board of directors, feel insecure when they have an errand to the house. They admit they would rather not go in alone.

But the house did not frighten the four children of Harriet Bennett Norton. They had come to the Ellsworth mansion in 1877 when their mother married Dighton (D. B.) Ellsworth a year after his first wife, Amanda, died. In fact, the four loved to play in the house.

Whenever D. B. and Harriet entertained in the parlor, Harriet's children were free to wander through the rest of the house. Sometimes they went down the back stairway, into the kitchen and pantry. While the servants were occupied with feeding the guests, the children stole from the kitchen down to the basement and came up into the backyard by way of the outside cellar steps. Their favorite place, though, was the tower.

It took some doing, but when the six children were all together at holiday time they used every chance to go up there. As soon as their mother left the house, they gathered at the top of the elegant curved stairway with its polished walnut balustrade. Pulling on their heaviest sweaters, they tiptoed through the storeroom and proceeded as usual up the narrower stairs to the tower room. Martin usually cleared the cobwebs away with the old broom. Lauraette often carried a lighted candle. George would help his stepsister Florence's small children, hardly able to climb the stairs themselves yet. Little Orinda (the others called her Rennie) squeezed up through the trapdoor square last, dragging her old doll with her. The tower or belvedere was not a major part of the structure, but it was impressive. Some said the windows on all four sides of the tower gave the house an airy and somewhat pretentious look.

Whatever its purpose, the four young Nortons accepted the challenge it presented. To them, it was the most interesting part of the house. They loved to look out over the town and imagine what it was like before their stepfather built the house in 1867 and before other early settlers like the Days, the Bucknells, the Landers, the Painters and Mrs. Hughes built their homes nearby.

During the winter of 1878–79, D. B. Ellsworth still operated a dry goods business down at the bottom of the hill, and gifts as well as supplies could be bought there. On that late December afternoon, when Harriet left the house to enlist her husband's help with the Christmas purchases, the servants were busy in the kitchen, making crumpets and plum pudding and other delicacies that graced the holiday tables of the English families in the community. Preparing those foods required the complete attention of the servants, and so the children once again made use of the chance to go up to the tower.

Once there, Lauraette set the candle on a ledge where its light reflected off the windows and bounced back and forth with the air currents from the stairs. It was a rule that the last one up had to leave the door at the bottom open, for the dim light that came up from the storeroom.

Because it was late afternoon in December and it was starting to snow, the tower was brightened only by the wavering, eerie light from the candle. That, along with the frost settling on the cold windows from the breathing of six children in the small space, resulted in a strange effect to anyone who chanced to look up from outside.

As Etta (Lauraette liked it when the others shortened her name) wiped a window clear so she could see out, she thought she saw someone waving to her. She was looking north across the street and west toward the octagon house at the other end of the block. When she was sure someone was there, she told the others. They thought they, too, could see someone on the lookout at the top of the other house. It looked like a man moving along heavily, unsteadily. At first, because of the distance between the houses and the bothersome frosting up of the tower windows, the figure looked more spirit-like than human. But when it waved its arms around, it looked much like a person about to fall over the railing. George asked, "But who could be out there in the cold? It doesn't even look like he has on a shirt or a coat."

Martin said, "I wonder if he wants us to help him down."

They wiped their hands back and forth on the cold windows again, and once more they saw someone waving back, even more frantically, it seemed.

Just as the children planned to leave their haunt and go across the street to help, they heard stomping downstairs and knew their parents would be in the front entrance, taking off their snowy boots and wraps. The six of them had all they could do to wriggle one by one through the opening in the floor, work their way cautiously down the steps, stow the candle and broom at the bottom, and remind Rennie to close the door before they met Mr. and Mrs. Ellsworth's inquisitive glances directed up toward them.

The adults thought they saw the shining eyes and bright cheeks of six darling youngsters all aglow with the excitement of the season and with curiosity about the queerly shaped bundles poking out in all directions from the shoppers' arms and coat pockets. Little did they know that the children had just spent another thrilling hour in the tower room that they couldn't mention for fear they might be scolded.

The children didn't reveal their secret until many years later, when it became known that an early occupant of the octagon house was frequently seen by others, too, in a red-nosed and very unsteady condition, out on the high lookout. Whenever that happened, it is said it took several men to go up there and persuade him to come back inside. He probably thought the children were waving to him that December afternoon, and they thought he was signaling for help. If he wasn't, they thought he was going to need it anyway, but they had to spend the rest of the evening hoping he got down safely without them. And Rennie had to go to sleep without her doll. She had forgotten to pick it up when they all started down in a hurry.

It is said there are bats in the belvedere now. Perhaps there are also ghosts of the people who lived there so long ago.

Perhaps Harriet's children sent their spirits back to haunt the dark stairway and the tower. Passersby sometimes think they see children waving from the frost-patterned windows.

Any house that is 120 years old is likely to boast its ghosts. The Ellsworth-Porter House, now the Porter House Museum, is one of those. But the ghosts are of a playful nature. That is why they are referred to as the Porter House ghosties.

A Sad Figure Appeared at Night

"I woke up not knowing what woke me. Not fifteen minutes had passed since I had put Curt down—for the night, I hoped. Now that he was six months old, I thought he might sleep all night—most of the time, at least."

Sheryl went on with her story. "We had been living in the house for a month or so. After we were settled there, we put Curt's crib in the wide hallway just outside our bedroom door. We could keep a close eye on him there if we left the bedroom door open.

"I wasn't really worried about leaving the crib out there. We felt safe in the house. But when I started waking up at night, my first thought was to listen for sounds from Curt, in case he had fussed or cried. I had no reason to think it was anything else that woke me.

"The second or third time it happened, I knew it wasn't Curt. He was always sleeping soundly. I started to get the feeling that someone or something was out in the hall. I knew I should get up and look or wake Ed up or turn on a light or something, but I hesitated.

"This all happened where we were living about twenty-five years ago. Shortly after Curt was born, we had moved to a town in the southern part of Butler County, where we rented a house that had once been a parsonage. At that time, we knew nothing about the history of the house, so we had no reason to feel concern.

"The strangest thing about it was that when I woke up at night,

I began to realize I was seeing a shape as if a person were standing over Curt's crib. The shape was fairly large, so I assumed it to be the shape or shadow of a man. But it had to be a ghost. There was no way anyone alive could be there in the hall, by our son's crib.

"If it was the ghost of a man, he never said anything or made any sound—he just stood there looking at Curt. Somehow, maybe because he was so quiet or maybe from his posture, I got the impression that he was sad. After a few minutes, he would disappear.

"I wasn't really scared of him, but after it happened a couple of times, I knew it was for real. I was sure I wasn't dreaming.

"One night when I saw the shape there in the hall, I tried to wake Ed. I nudged him as soon as the figure appeared. I whispered, 'Ed, there he is again!' But Ed never saw him. By the time he woke up wide, the ghost was always gone.

"This kept happening every couple of weeks or so, all the time we lived there.

"I can't describe his features or say definitely that he looked sad. It was always night, and it must have been the street light on the corner just outside our bedroom window that helped me to even see him. From the bed, I could see through the doorway directly to the crib.

"Later on we found out that the house had been remodeled before we moved in. We think the inside stairway to the second floor was taken out at that time, leaving that nice, wide hallway.

"But the time came for us to move again. After we lived in that house for about six months, Ed's job took us to another state. We've lived in several different houses since then, but I haven't been wakened by a ghost or seen one since, so I guess the ghost was connected to that house in Butler County and didn't follow us to our other homes.

"Ed finally came to believe my story, though. About ten years after we moved out of that house, a member of my family showed me a reprint of an old newspaper article. It told of a tragic incident that had occurred there. According to the article, about eleven o'clock one night many years ago, after a family argument earlier that evening, the son of the minister took the rifle and shot and killed his father in the small upper hallway. He confessed the next day that he also shot and seriously injured his mother.

"Even though ten years had passed by the time we read the article, the earlier incidents from the time we lived in that same house came back to mind, only much more clearly. We think the ghost of the murdered father came back to the scene of the tragic crime. We think he was either still trying to figure out what had happened and why, or trying to relive the happier times when his own son was an innocent baby. Even if it was our son he looked down on there in the crib, perhaps he was finally able to feel close to his son again."

The Skeleton's Hand

The house was in National, in the Garnavillo area, which boasts of perhaps the richest, blackest land in Clayton County. Once a thriving community, National is now only a small gathering of houses.

But the house did—maybe still does—exist. Or so a local man says his grandfather, now dead, told him. His grandfather was a great storyteller, and this story, which happened about 1910, was one he swore was true.

The elegant two-story brick home and the land had been owned by a doctor before the Hans Neyerman family bought the farm. The doctor had a good practice and was by all accounts an excellent medical man. He was also a bit eccentric. Because there were few laws regarding burials then, the bodies of the poor and of criminals who died were often used by the medical profession to learn about the human body and its ailments. Somehow, during his years of medical practice, the doctor had obtained a skeleton that he insisted was that of a famous criminal. He kept this ghoulish item in an upstairs bedroom closet and frequently brought it out for his guests to view, whether they wanted to or not. He would only laugh when they cringed, saying, "It's only the live ones you have to worry about!"

Hans Neyerman and his family—wife, two boys, and three girls—bought the farm in late 1909. The doctor's health was declining and by spring, when the Neyermans were to move, the doctor had died. The doctor's wife took the lovely furniture and the thick velvet drapes from the arched windows, but she left the skeleton. She had always hated it, she told Hans, and he was welcome to it.

Hans did not really want the skeleton either, but he had much to do and he could not bury the skeleton when the ground was still frozen. But he assured his wife, Augusta, that he would move it as soon as spring came. He would give the skeleton a decent burial in the small private plot on the farm.

The children at first would not go near the room at the top of the stairs. This bedroom was used as a storeroom. But gradually the children started to peek into the room, then quickly retreat. They began to stay a little longer until they were all boldly entering the room (though only in the daytime) and playing there. All except Marie, the youngest. She was seven and did not like the bedroom or the closet or anything in the "scare room." In the evenings, the children would complain the room was too chilly and dark to play in, even though it was lit with candles as the other rooms were.

The family got used to the house and, despite Hans's promises, he did not get the skeleton removed and buried. Marie had a birthday this June and wanted to have a party. Hans thought a party an extravagance, but he had a soft spot for his youngest and finally consented, promising her he would have the skeleton out before her birthday in two weeks. However, the day before the party, it rained hard and Hans couldn't bury the skeleton.

Eight little boys and girls arrived in their parents' buggies and wagons, the girls in long dresses and the boys in knickers. First to arrive was Karine, a fair-skinned girl with blond straight hair. She was Marie's best friend. Karine's parents were Norwegian, unusual in this solid German community, and Karine was teased because of her Scandinavian accent. But today she was very happy because her mother had let her wear a special outfit. She had on a red and white Norwegian costume, hand-embroidered by her grandmother. Marie thought the outfit was beautiful.

After eating cake, the children played games. Never having been in the house before, they wanted to play hide and seek so they could explore this fancy home. They had also heard about the skeleton from their parents, though Marie would never talk about it.

Reluctantly, Augusta gave permission—if they were careful—and they were not to go upstairs. Marie started the game and, several turns later, she was "it" again. Even though she was not supposed to, Karine's curiosity got the better of her and she snuck up the oak staircase. She crouched down to peer at Marie through the railing. When Marie got to "eight," Karine slipped into the first room she saw, at the top of the stairs. The door was slightly ajar. Despite the fact it was June, the day had become dark; the storm clouds of the day before were returning. By now, Karine could hear Marie saying "ten!"

In the gloomy room, Karine could see a small bed against the opposite wall. A dresser was on her left and a rag rug covered the shiny wood floor. Karine could just make out a door near the foot of the bed. As she started toward this door, thunder boomed and she jumped back. She remembered seeing a lighted candle on a table in the hallway. She ducked back out, took the candle, and set it on the dresser in the room. The soft glow made her feel better. Taking off her red cap, she set it carefully on the dresser and walked towards the closet door.

By this time, Marie had found all the other children and, giving up, hollered for Karine to come out. But Karine did not come. They quickly searched the downstairs and decided to ask Mrs. Neyerman. Augusta started to look but suddenly spied the light under the closet door at the top of the stairs just as Karine screamed. Augusta ran up the steps with Marie and the other children following. As they opened the door, they saw Karine, white and shaking, stagger out of the closet and collapse.

Augusta rushed to her and lifted up her head, instructing one of the boys to get Hans and to tell him to get a doctor.

"He grabbed me, he grabbed me. He wouldn't let go," Karine whispered. Her eyes rolled back and she went limp. "Who?" asked Augusta, shaking the small body gently.

"Him, Mommy," said Marie, pointing to the closet. And there was the skeleton, long blond strands of hair in its right hand.

By the time the doctor arrived, Karine had died. The doctor said she died of heart failure. He thought she may have had a weak heart and the shock of the incident killed her. Hans removed the skeleton and buried it in an unmarked grave. Augusta locked the door to the closet and to the room. The family never used the room again.

The man who told this story does not recall the precise spot his grandfather said the house stood. The house may still be there, doors locked.

A Small Witch

Vera was very young at the turn of the twentieth century. Throughout her whole life she was a fairly short person. As she said, "I started out small."

When Vera was old enough to sing in the children's choir, she didn't have far to walk from the Decorah Public School to the Congregational United Church of Christ for choir practice; it was practically on her way home. She and her friend Margaret would walk together.

One Wednesday in late October, Julie Ann, the young choir director, let them sing a couple of fun songs after they perfected the one for the next Sunday's service. She had even put up Halloween decorations and provided big suckers.

After practice, Julie said to the children, "I'm glad some of you stayed to help clean up. You can take the decorations home to put in your own windows, if you want to." By the time the last ones scrambled for the decorations and pulled fuzzy woolen sweaters on over their sticky hands and faces, it was near dusk.

Vera's friend Margaret wasn't at practice that day. She had missed school, too. Vera found herself wishing she didn't have to walk home alone. She thought of the songs they had been singing, and decided she could be brave as she left the church.

When she reached the corner where the Decorah Public Library is now, she looked down the hill toward the railroad tracks. Good luck—there was no train at the crossing.

Thankful that she wouldn't have to wait for a train, young Vera walked to the bottom of the hill. At the next intersection, she waited for a freight wagon to go by before she crossed the street. She was thinking about what she could do with the big black paper spooks and toothy orange jack-o'-lanterns she was carrying.

Looking ahead toward home, Vera saw a figure that filled her with fear. It had the same shape as the paper spooks she had in her hand. But this live, moving spook clutched a black shawl tightly around its shoulders with one hand, and with the other it tapped the sidewalk with a long, gnarled stick.

With a live spook coming right toward her, Vera found it hard to be brave. It seemed they would meet face to face on the railroad crossing. Trembling, Vera tried to think what to do. Just as she reached the crossing, the dark figure turned right, onto the flagstone path to the door of the old stone house. There it disappeared.

Watching every movement at the door and windows as she scurried by, Vera realized that she had just seen the witch who lived all alone in that old house.

Vera recalled her fears that late October afternoon. "She was as tall as I am, and half as wide," she said, "so she was a fairly small witch. My friends and I began to watch for her. We discovered that she came out regularly, just at dusk, to walk. She always wore that black shawl, and she carried that twisted walking stick. She never talked. Just walked. We never knew where to."

At that time, the house stood on the north side of the Decorah street now called East Broadway. It was at about the point where the tracks angled across town to Water Street, just before they crossed over onto "The Flat." The house is gone now. But at the time of Vera's scare, the original stone part had stood since about 1855. During the

Civil War, wooden structures were added on the west side. When the wood fences used for many years as dams went down from the force of the Upper Iowa River in flood stage, the house had about four feet of water on the first floor. The little lady who lived there was used to climbing the stairs to the second floor until the muddy water subsided.

The Solitary Crucifix

In the late 1880s, there stood a house a few miles south of Thompson Corners, which is between Lansing and Harpers Ferry in Allamakee County. The house was near the Paint Rock Church, later organized as St. Joseph's Church of Harpers Ferry. The church was torn down in 1976, although a cemetery and chapel remain at the church site.

This story, told by Madonna Storla of Postville, is one she remembers her grandmother telling. It involves both the house and the Paint Rock Church. The massive 3,000-pound bell, installed in August 1889, would peal to remind the hard-working pioneer parishioners of their Sunday services.

The Paint Rock Church, built in the late 1860s or 1870s, was named for the unusual painted rock on the Mississippi River. This rock was first mentioned by explorers in 1817 and was old even then. The bluff on which Paint Rock is found is one of several nearly vertical faces of rock and is about six miles from the site of the Paint Rock Church. A narrow shelf of rock runs high along the face, and Native Americans years ago painted the rock with red dye. This rock was said to be considered sacred by the Native Americans.

Living in the house near the church was a man called Mr. Banks. He was an evil-tempered man with a quiet, gentle wife and one child, a son. Banks's wife was a devout Catholic, but he refused to let her or their son attend church. As time went on, he became even more eccentric. Coming out of the house on Sundays he would yell insults and blasphemies at the parishioners on their way to church. Upset, they spoke to their parish priest, who decided to talk to a local member. He chose Mrs. Sconlon, whose parents had been early settlers and who had known Mrs. Banks before her marriage.

"Well, Father, what can I do for you?"

"I would like to speak to Mr. Banks about his behavior. Since I know so little of him, I thought you could help me. What can you tell me about the family?"

"Ahhh, Father, the things I can tell! Mrs. Banks—such a pretty and shy thing she was, still is. And so devout, Father! She never missed her church day, not least till she took up with him." She leaned forward. "I told her he was no good. They say he's, well, you know," and she tapped her temple.

"Mrs. Sconlon, we don't know that."

"Anybody acts the way he does, I believe it. He just likes to sit at home and think about himself. He don't care about her or the boy."

"Mrs. Sconlon..."

"It's true, Father. She don't never get to go to town—and you seen how he acts about church. Last time I was to see her, he was rude to me. Said I talked too much. Said I was an old busybody! To my face!"

The priest coughed loudly. "He did?"

"Yes, he did. You'll be needin' some medicine for that cough, Father. But before he got there, I had a visit with Mrs. Banks—we use to be real close. Told her all about what we're doin' in church and the new bell that come and all." Mrs. Sconlon paused for a moment. "You know what, Father?"

"What?"

"You don't tell nobody 'cause she told me not to tell, but you bein' a priest and all, well, it's okay."

"Yes."

"Well, she done got a crucifix!"

The priest stared at her. "Where?"

"In her bedroom. They got separate rooms, you know, her and him. She got hold of some paper or somethin' and she cut out a picture of a crucifix. Has it beside her bed, nailed to the wall. He, Mr. Banks that is, don't like it none too well. But she leaves it up. Now ain't that somethin'!"

The priest looked at her thoughtfully. "Yes, Mrs. Sconlon, that's somethin'!"

The next day the priest went to see the Banks family. He never got past the door. He had barely stepped on the property when Mr. Banks stormed out, bellowing, "GET OFF MY PROPERTY!"

The priest tried to explain why he came. Mr. Banks just kept yelling. He and the priest argued, but when Banks grabbed for his shotgun, the priest left.

The following Sunday was rainy, a dark, dreary sort of day. As members of the congregation trudged past the Bankses' home and up the hill from Harpers Ferry, they were shocked to see Mr. Banks standing on the porch of his house, railing against the priest, the church, and God. The rain began to increase, pouring down steadily, and low thunder could be heard. As the lightning flashed, they could see Banks gesturing and pointing to the sky, the sound of rain and thunder drowning out his words.

People were nearly running past the house now. Some said they saw Mr. Banks grab his gun before he leaped off the porch. Suddenly there was a loud crack and a lightning bolt struck the ground near the house. The bolt was so bright it dazzled the parishioners and, for a few moments, they could not see. Then they heard Mrs. Banks screaming. Some of the men rushed to help her and others went to the church to fetch the priest.

When he arrived, several men had already carried Banks into

the house. His body lay on the floor, covered with a blanket. Banks was dead, struck by the bolt of lightning. The house suffered some damage and the plaster had been knocked off all the walls. Mrs. Sconlon took Mrs. Banks to her bedroom and then the group outside heard another scream. Rushing to the bedroom, the priest was puzzled until he saw both women looking at one wall. There was no plaster left on any of the walls, except for a tiny patch of it by the bed. There was a picture of a crucifix nailed to it.

Mrs. Banks lived in the house a short while, but it was not a happy home. She left the area and never came back. The house stood vacant, but people told stories of seeing ghostly, flickering lights in the windows of the abandoned home. In the winter, people passing by heard snow crunching or saw footprints in the snow with no one around to make them.

The house withstood the weather for many years, but finally crumbled away, except for one wall of the old bedroom. When the remains of the house were finally hauled away, that wall, with the faded crucifix picture still attached, had to be torn down. After the house was gone, the area became part of a peaceful green pasture and has not been haunted since.

The Solitary Crucifix

Someone was Jumping on Me

"1308 Fifth Street doesn't sound very ominous, does it?"

With that question, Craig began his story. He said, "Well, for at least one spring day, it was ominous, for me. You see, I had come home for the week, to study. While I was there, I was staying in my room in the basement. With not much else going on other than studying for exams, it was generally a pretty dead week in that quiet town not far from the center of Iowa. Even the family pets, our two dogs, kept quiet up on first floor while I was down there studying. But then, unexpectedly, something strange happened to upset the peace and quiet—at least, for me, and maybe for the dogs—for a very short time.

"I was sleeping in my bed down there one of those nights, when I was suddenly awakened by someone shaking me. At first, I thought that it was my younger brother and his friend pushing on the waterbed mattress. But then I realized I was stuck down into the waterbed and could hardly move. I threatened them. At least, I threatened who I thought it was, in no uncertain words.

"No one spoke up or answered me in any way. When I opened my eyes, I saw nothing unusual, and I was really puzzled. I couldn't move my body. A weight rested on my chest. It felt as if someone had been jumping on me, and then stayed there. In that moment of fright, I called out for my Grandmother Evie to help me.

"Grandma Evie had passed away a number of years earlier, after a bout with cancer. Though I don't remember her ever having lived in that house—in fact, I know she never had—I found myself calling out for her to help me. I must have sensed her presence, somehow, watching over me as she would have done when I was small, and before she took sick. Maybe it was because I had called out to her rather loudly that the shaking and the feeling that someone was jumping on me stopped.

"I got up from the bed then and went upstairs. Up there, I saw a red glowing mass for just an instant. It had no particular shape. It was between the dining area and the living room when I saw it. The dogs were behind me when I went through the patio doorway into the screened-in porch and out onto the deck. They had been barking at something I couldn't see. There was no one outside, and I could see nothing that would account for what had just happened inside or anything that could have set the dogs to barking. Then they both came on out to the screened-in porch and quit barking.

"I didn't go back into the house for about an hour. Then I decided that whatever it was, the incident was over. But I never did figure out what was going on there. Even thinking it all through again, I still don't have a clue. I just know I don't want anything like it to happen again, exams or no exams to study for.

"I packed my bag and went back to Ames to study there. It took over a year for me to get over the feelings of fright and insecurity I had felt down there in my room in the basement at home. I had recurring nightmares over it, for some time afterward.

"Later on, a friend said, 'Craig, when I slept on the couch downstairs in that same house, the same sort of thing happened to me.' I didn't want to take the chance of going through that experience again, so I sort of fortified myself for anything like it, whenever I slept downstairs at home again, so it never happened to me again. I'm glad of that. That first time shook me up enough!"

Spook Hollow House

Wallace and April Finnegan decided that whether the "spook" had left or not, memories of the event definitely had not. So their Spook Hollow house, on the Skip Level Road, was burned. The old house sat just outside Millville, a small town in southeast Clayton County, not far from Guttenberg. The Colesburg Fire Department burned the house for practice on a sunny October day in 1986. Even though the physical evidence is gone, those memories still linger on.

It was 1959, Thanksgiving Day, when 83-year-old William Meyer and his 77-year-old wife, Anna, awoke covered with a fine dust. The weather had been unusually cold before Thanksgiving and the wood frame house had been contracting and expanding with loud cracks and pops. Although the family thought this peculiar, they were not alarmed. After all, as a young man Mr. Meyer had helped his father build this very house and he knew it was sound. But the dust worried them. The ceilings were tight and the plaster was not cracked. Still the bedroom and living room were covered with a thin layer of whitish dust. This was only the beginning.

In the next three weeks, a well-stocked, heavy refrigerator in the pantry tipped over, smashing dishes on a shelf. An upstairs window shattered, with glass falling equally inside and outside the frame. A pedestal for a flower pot shot across a room and hit the cookstove. And Anna was hit on the head by a glass that suddenly fell from a sturdy shelf.

William, bedridden with a hip ailment, and Anna were solid German folk, not given to fantasies. But they were getting scared now. To prove to themselves there really was nothing going on, they devised a test. They set an egg on top of a small lamp chimney, knowing the slightest movement would cause the egg to fall. With their grandson, they sat and watched the egg for an hour. Nothing happened. With a feeling of relief, they decided to go to bed. Because of Mr. Meyer's hip, it took a little longer to turn in for the night. They had just settled down when they heard a loud noise. Mrs. Meyer rushed to the living room to find the egg smashed and dripping from a doorway across the room. That was enough for them. Even though Mr. Meyer had lived on this farm all his life and in this home all of his married life, he knew they had to leave. In mid-December 1959, Mr. and Mrs. Meyer moved from their six-room white house with the well-polished floors and neatly kept lawn. They went to live with Mr. Meyer's brother in Guttenberg. They never returned.

Different theories were put forth by people after these events were publicized by the media. The sheriff of Clayton County thought vandals were at work. Or he did until he and two others were examining the home and a bottle leaped from a packing crate to the floor. A relative and another friend went to the home to collect the last household goods; one of these was a rocking chair that started to rock without their help. They held the arms and stopped the chair, but as soon as they let go, the chair began to rock again. A reporter, also dubious, was checking the house for a story when a large limestone rock tore loose from the basement wall and smashed a ten-gallon stone crock.

The most popular theory was that underground water pressure caused the strange happenings. Elmer Meyer, son of William and Anna, doused the yard and said water was running in underground crevices forty feet below a front corner of the house. A spring came up on one side of the house and a creek ran on the other, so water was nearby. Relatives of the family felt that water pressure was building up and that this was responsible for the incidents, most of which occurred in the front part of the house. Others said water pressure combined with static electricity caused the events.

Continued interest in the house and the "water theory" versus the "ghost theory" led to growing interest from scientists. Duke University's Dr. J. G. Pratt, professor of parapsychology, was so interested he called the sheriff every day for a week. The state colleges got interested, too, and set January 8, 1960, as "ghost test" night. Students and professors from Upper Iowa, Fayette, and students from what is now the University of Iowa at Iowa City showed up in early afternoon. The Upper Iowa group came equipped with an ion counter, an argon radiation counter to determine if any underground faults existed, a Geiger counter, and an oscilloscope to check for electromagnetic fields. The University of Iowa students brought no equipment but kept watch upstairs.

However, the test night had gotten coverage well in advance of the event. As a result, the house was packed with students, professors, newsmen, and neighbors. Outside the house an unruly group of spectators started pounding on the doors and poking their heads in at windows. Those inside the house were concerned about the effect any more people, especially this restless group, would have on the experiment. They locked all doors. This led to yelled insults from the crowd outside, and a near-riot ensued. Increased pounding on the doors and yelling put everyone inside on edge. The inside group decided to jerk open the doors and shine flashlights into the crowd. This made the outsiders angry and they broke down a basement door. After much protest, the mob finally dispersed and the testers settled down to their experiment. At 3:00 am all house lights were turned off, and all was quiet until 5:00 am, when a reporter fell asleep and began to snore. The professors and students left the morning of

January 9 to analyze their instrument readings. After all results were added up, they totaled almost zero. All instruments registered normal except the ion counter, which recorded an unusually high negative ion count at the outset of the test. Later this leveled off to a normal reading. Was something there and then left? There were no conclusive results.

Shortly after the test night, another professor visited the home and stated the strange happenings were the result of some "intelligence." He also said this could mean practical jokers or other forces.

As many as 2,000 people were coming to the house on weekends, and the sheriff was making the thirty-seven-mile trip from Elkader frequently. Barriers were finally put up and the road was blocked off, but tourists still got through.

William and Anna Meyer wanted nothing more to do with the property. They sold it in May of 1960 to Wallace and April Finnegan. The house was never occupied again and was used for several years as hay storage. Tourists still tried to visit the home, and the Finnegans were forced to put up a gate and a "dead end" sign to discourage them.

Gradually interest died and the tourists stopped coming. But every year, especially at Halloween, people would turn up to see the Spook Hollow house and reporters would call. The Finnegans say they never had any problems with ghosts or ghostly events in the years they owned the property.

So was there a poltergeist or not? No explanation was ever found. The Meyer family was never troubled with any ghostly problems again. And one of the professors said it was uncommon for a poltergeist to remain in and be active in an empty house. Did the ghost, if there was one, eventually find another home? Or did it live on in that deserted house until the fire of October 1986? There are still no answers. Only questions.

A Strange, Unseen Force

My requests for ghost stories brought a variety of responses. Some of the stories that were offered for the collections have been the type expected: they were about unexplainable happenings or incidents involving a ghost, a presence, a spirit, or a poltergeist. Some were about a force—some kind of energy that resulted in some kind of action. The resulting action could be seen or felt, but not the force.

Those who told these stories thought possibly some kind of electrical energy was present at that time and location to cause the action. I've heard of this before, from people it happened to. I can't explain it; I can only pass their stories on to my readers.

Brenda Kahl had such a story. She said that almost fifteen years ago, while she was living in Stanwood, she and her roommate (I'll call her Grace) were returning home. Grace had told Brenda about a reportedly haunted farm house where a woman and her daughter had died in a house fire quite a lot earlier. After the fire, passersby reported seeing a light on in the attic. Brenda said, "That's why I asked Grace to take me by it."

But they had to make a stop first at Grace's mother's house, to drop off a card table. Brenda said, "Grace's mom was thinking right when she reminded us to be careful. We hadn't even told her where we were going on our way home. But when we got back in the car, we locked both back doors and went on our way. We had to go around a corner to go on up the hill where the house is. When we turned the corner, we didn't see a light in the attic, but both back car doors flew open. Figure that one out!"

They've Always Been With Us

Inga has been seeing ghosts or spirits since the day she moved to the old farmhouse in the northeast Iowa countryside as a new bride in 1979. That very first night, surrounded by wedding gifts, she glanced outside and saw a man standing in the yard, wearing a long black coat. A few moments later, she saw the same man on the other side of the yard. Her husband had gone to town to get a few more things and they didn't even have curtains on the windows. Inga was so terrified that she hurriedly opened up gifts until she found a set of knives and sat in the middle of the gifts, clutching a knife. When she told her husband, he suggested she was just overly tired. She did her best to forget about the episode.

Months later, though, she saw a glimpse of the same man going up the stairs from the kitchen and later from a bedroom to the attic. She was still scared, but curious. During the times she saw the man, he did not seem to emanate evil and she did not feel threatened. Instead, he just seemed to be walking around. She never saw his face, for he wore the long black coat and a black hat. Often she would hear someone come in and sit down on a chair in the kitchen, but after getting up and checking, she found no one there. One time she heard snoring next to her in bed, although her husband was not in bed with her. Her daughters had also heard the sounds of someone breathing loudly.

After checking with neighbors, she found out that a man had died of a stroke in the yard on the farm. His family was a bit peculiar and, while waiting for the doctor, they draped a long black coat over him and left him in the yard. Inga also found out this was just one of many stories about her new home.

The family that had lived in the home before Inga and her family had moved from another small salt-box-type home and built this one. Although the family had five children, none of them married and they all lived together in the house. One brother died of the flu in his twenties. Inga said they found a letter in the attic from the young man, and it was obvious he knew he was going to die. She does not know what happened to the letter. Another brother was the one who died of a stroke on the lawn. Then there was the sister who was at the well or cistern getting water when she fell in and drowned. However, dark rumors also suggest that she had jumped into the well.

About ten years after her marriage, Inga saw a young girl, about five or six years old. She remembers vividly the first time she saw the little girl. Inga was sitting in the dining room one cold Saturday in January, doing book work. She looked up and saw a small girl, skipping into the room from the kitchen. The girl paused and looked at Inga and Inga looked back. To this day, Inga remembers the little girl was wearing a dusky blue dress with white flowers, and she wore high-top boots. Her long, light brown hair fell around her shoulders and she had a big bow in her hair to match her dress. She suddenly skipped away and was gone. A different time, Inga heard giggles and girlish laughter from the house when her own daughters were not in the house. Later on, the youngest daughter, six at the time, came to her mother and said a girl had just come skipping into the dining room and looked at her. Another time a different daughter saw a little girl kneeling in front of the stuffed bear the family kept in the upstairs hallway.

About a year ago the upstairs toilet stopped working. One day it was functioning and the next day it wasn't. A plumber paid a visit and after checking it out, he wanted to know why they had removed all the plumbing parts from the tank. The family was astonished when the plumber lifted the tank cover: the inside was completely empty.

At times, Inga would put her car keys in the place where she always kept them, and the next day they would be gone. They might be in a cupboard or hidden behind a canister. Another time Inga put down her makeup bag and stepped out of the room. When she came back, it was gone. She went downstairs to see if it was there, and when she returned upstairs the bag was right where it should have been. A hairbrush and curling iron disappeared and reappeared, too. Were these tricks played by the little girl?

When an elderly neighbor showed Inga a confirmation picture of the woman who had drowned in the well, Inga recognized the girl in the picture as her ghostly visitor, even though the confirmation picture showed a girl of thirteen or fourteen.

Despite the fact that the family does not feel the spirits are malevolent, none of the children will stay in the house alone and Inga feels uneasy when alone. Her husband has never seen any of these ghostly visitors, and is somewhat skeptical of them, despite the stories from his wife and daughters. Inga feels he does not see the apparitions because he does not let himself see them. The family does not plan on moving from their scenic northeast Iowa farm, with its rolling hills and valleys, but Inga and her daughters are always on the lookout for any ghosts.

Tricked _by a_ Troll

Some people say they have seen or sensed the presence of ghosts. And many people of Scandinavian descent say they have seen or felt the presence of trolls—troublesome beings. Trolls live in all of northeast Iowa, but most of the stories about these Norwegian imports center around Decorah.

There are several kinds of trolls. Water trolls live in the Upper Iowa River and numerous creeks and streams. Bridge trolls live under College Drive Bridge or the Tavener Bridge near Pulpit Rock. Large wood trolls and rock trolls with their square, flat heads live in the woods and parks—Palisades Park, Dunning's Spring, Phelps Park, and Malanaphy Springs, to name a few. The trolls may live anywhere, but their headquarters is Ice Cave, just north of Decorah.

All trolls are ugly, but people say the water trolls, with their light green, slippery, slimy hair are the ugliest. They spend most of their time under water, with only their hair floating on the surface. Occasionally, their bulging, dark eyes can be seen peeping out from the water.

Our story concerns Lars Larson and his encounter with these mischievous creatures. One day Lars decided he wanted to go fishing. He probably should have gone to work, but it was a clear, sunny summer day. So instead he took his fishing pole and tackle box and headed for a new, secret fishing spot on a small stream that fed into the Upper Iowa. He had found the spot over a month ago, but this would be his first chance to fish it.

Lars parked his car on the road and started the long walk to the creek. While trying to avoid a wall of tall weeds, he brushed by a patch of gooseberry bushes and ripped a hole in his pants. Then he tripped not once but twice over large rocks he did not remember from his first visit.

When Lars reached the creek, he baited his hook and fished from a small, wooden bridge. To the right was a marshy area with cattails and assorted water-loving weeds. Lars was sure there were fish just waiting to be caught in this secret spot. No sooner had he thrown his line in than he felt a tug. Pulling hard, he found a rusty tin can on the end of the line. Lars was removing the tin can when he saw the cattails on his right whipping back and forth. He studied the area. The movement stopped. Just weeds—or had he seen something else? Wondering, he baited his hook again and settled back. The sun was high and hot now and he was getting drowsy. A powerful jerk pulled the pole almost out of his hands. Struggling to hold on, Lars braced his feet against the side of the bridge and leaned back. But the bridge was old and shaky and Lars was yanked through the rotted railings and off the bridge.

He landed in a deep pocket in the stream and fought to get to the surface. He could see what looked like light green weeds all around him, and he was tangled up in it. Lars felt as though the weeds were really a thousand fingers, pulling him down. At last he struggled free and stood upright in the shallow part of the creek. Lars heard a laugh and turned around to see two black, fish-like eyes duck under the water. The green seaweed moved rapidly down the stream, with his line and pole attached.

Lars was shaking, and not just from the cold water. He went home immediately. Lars vowed he would never skip work again to go fishing. Only he and the water troll knew the reason why.

Was "It" Sent by Mary Jane?

Leann said it all started one fall when her daughters Carla and Marla came home to Lake Park for the winter. During the summer, they had rented a place in Spirit Lake so they could be nearer their work at Arnolds Park. Marla was about twenty then, and Carla was about eighteen.

Their first night home, Carla dreamt that a bird hit the window and broke it. "When I asked her if she checked the window," Leann said, "she went back to the larger upstairs room where she had been sleeping. Sure enough, the one window in that room was broken. The big piece of glass that broke loose fell to the inside, so we figured something from the outside had broken it. But...a bird?"

Leann said that the very next night, Carla slept in the smaller room upstairs. Sounds woke her again. As she glanced toward the doorway to the larger room, she saw the figure of a man standing there with a knife in his hand."Carla is a determined person, so she went on downstairs. But when we talked about it, we all realized the figure she saw was identical to one she had drawn for an art class in school. That was pretty scary.

"It seems that a lot of unexplainable things went on in that house from then on, and we fell into the habit of putting the blame on 'It'—whatever it was."

Leann went on with the story. "Because Carla worked at night, she was used to doing her laundry in the daytime. One day Carla had a scary experience down in our basement. The rest of us were all working away from home at the time. She took her armful of clothes down there to put it in the washing machine. When she approached the washer, there was already hot water in it, and the water just churned and bubbled right up. It scared her so much that she threw the clothes in all at once. Just as suddenly, the bubbling stopped."

By then, the whole family knew something was going on in that house—something very strange. Whatever it was didn't bother Leann's husband, Tom, at all. It did bother Leann, but just once. She had taken their two younger children upstairs. She laid down with them so they could get to sleep, because she knew they were frightened in that house. Shortly after she fell asleep, Leann woke up hearing the banister squeaking. "It never ever squeaked otherwise," Leann said. "Carla and a friend of hers were in the next room. I tried to call to them to ask if they heard the same sound, but something had me bound so tight that I couldn't move. After about three tries to call out for help, I could only whisper, 'Carla....,' but they heard me and came out to see what I wanted. I still can't figure out what made me feel so bound up. There was nothing physical or visible there. It was more as if a force or a presence kept me from calling out. I took my pillow with me and went back downstairs to finish my sleep.

"One night Tom and I went out for supper. When we returned, Carla was standing in the front doorway trying to flag down her sister and her boyfriend as they went by. That time, what had scared her was that the kitchen light had gone out. First she thought the bulb had burned out, but when she flipped the switch it came back on. She couldn't leave the house to get help, because her two younger brothers and her little sister were sleeping on the couch. But she knew the kitchen light had been on until it mysteriously went off, and she wondered who or what had done that."

Leann thought back over all the happenings. She said, "Carla thought that light being turned off was about the last straw! After that, for weeks—probably more like months—we all slept on mattresses on the floor down in the large front room. It was hard to get our furniture up that narrow stairway anyway, so we had placed our own bed and some other furniture in the far end of the front room.

"But then while we slept downstairs, whatever it was started coming down the stairs, too, to bother us. The steps were carpeted, but we could hear the heavy footsteps coming down and going up.

"One night, Carla came home late and couldn't get to sleep because of the heavy footsteps walking all around her on the floor. She woke me so she could get to sleep, because (she said) nothing ever happened when I was awake. Every time I started to fall asleep again that night, Carla would say, 'Mom, you're falling asleep!' Sure I was! I'd been working since early morning and I was tired!

"One early morning before I got up for work, Carla heard the footsteps coming down the stairs. She just lay still by the couch. But whatever strange presence was in our house came toward her and hit her on her knees, as if something fell on her. Then 'It' went back upstairs—just as noisily. The next day, Carla had a bruise on both knees, where they would knock together. But when I got up to go to work, I didn't see anything there that could have been thrown down at her.

"One night, Tom came home late and stretched out on a mattress on the floor. Marla came home even later. She didn't want to chance going upstairs to sleep, so I said she could lie in bed with me because Dad would probably sleep all night right where he was. Before Marla fell asleep, she heard the heavy footsteps coming down. She looked up and saw a male figure. He sort of peeked around the end of the stairway wall and gave her a little wave before he went back upstairs.

"Marla woke me and wanted me to get up and check it out. She said, 'Mom, I think Dale John came home.' So I just went back to sleep, because that was fine with me. He was one of our boys. The next day when she told me what she saw that night, I realized she had been too scared to tell me. Our bed was in the big room on one side, and the front room on the other end, so we could see the front door real plain. No one had gone in or out that night.

"Almost all of us were affected by 'It' at one time or another. Dale John saw shadows like a black-clothed figure at the foot of his bed once. Tom heard a ruckus up there and hollered up, 'What's going on up there?' but it was Dale John shaking the bedpost and hollering, trying to scare 'It' away.

"Vertues heard the noises a lot, too. He tried to shut them out. When he was five or six, he said he just pushed his cheeks up with his hands and pulled his ears down so he couldn't hear them.

"Mike, our youngest, heard all the things the rest of us were telling about 'It,' so he was always expecting to see something or have something happen to him, but it didn't.

"The kids thought maybe someone was fooling around in the big storage space over the kitchen, trying to scare them. They asked the police to check it out. When they came over, they saw that the dust had been disturbed a little, but they did not see anything else that could account for what had been happening.

"I never liked to talk about these incidents and feelings," Leann said. "It seemed like whenever I did, 'It' didn't like it and would start something else happening to frighten us. When I talked it all over with Carla once again, she said, 'Well, Mom, I had been out at the Loon Lake Cemetery with some other kids that one night, before all this started. And people believe that if you're out there and walk on Mary Jane's grave or do anything else to desecrate her burial place, something bad will happen to you. They say it's the curse of a witch. Like those kids that had been out there messing around once, and shortly afterward were killed in a car accident. Maybe one of us walked on the wrong grave that night.'"

All these things happened about twenty years ago. Leann recalled, "Our house was next to the former D-X Station in Lake Park. Since then, the house has been buried. Maybe the ghost was buried with it!"

At least, nothing that can be blamed on "It" has happened yet in the house Leann and Tom live in now.

Who Moved *the* Bed Across *the* Room?

Andrea Gibbs said, "We hadn't heard the rumors until the day we moved in. A little boy shouted from across the street to ask if we knew the house was haunted."

The previous owners, Michael and Lynne Thompson of Davenport, bought the ten-room house in 1976. By then, the once beautiful trees and other plantings in the spacious yard had grown into a tangle. The house and its tower had also been neglected. The Thompsons did some renovating first. Then they moved in, and they continued what became for them a ten-year restoration project.

The house, an Italian villa style, was built in 1858 on a bluff in southwest Davenport. By the time Lynne Thompson was a young girl, she thought of the old house with its overgrown yard as "spooky." But that became a reality when she later lived in it.

Lynne said she heard doors opening and closing when she was alone in the house. They heard footsteps that weren't theirs. Lynne sometimes smelled perfume that no one in the house was wearing.

Once, Lynne heard someone screaming. She called out to her husband, "Mike—was that someone screaming on TV?"

He answered, "Nothing like that on the TV. If you heard someone screaming, maybe it was outside."

But after checking, neither of them could explain where that screaming came from.

The most unusual occurrence happened one night when the Thompsons were asleep in their bedroom. During that night, they woke up to the sound of something heavy being dragged—as if across the floor. Lynne thought it must be something outside. When they looked out the window, they saw nothing to explain the sound. The next morning, when they were wider awake, they both realized they shouldn't have been able to look out the window from next to the bed. Then they saw that their bed was across the room from where it had been when they went to bed the night before.

Lynne Thompson feels that "the ghosts were friendly—as if they liked knowing their house was being fixed up, so they approved the changes."

But what would account for the ghosts? Who were they? What part did they play in the history of the house?

Thomas Wilkinson, a building contractor, built the mansion in 1858. For many years, he worked hard to beautify the property. In 1876, after suffering from poor health, a pain in his spine, financial losses and a possible law suit, he killed himself. It was on Sunday morning, December 24.

His wife, Ellen, told the authorities that shortly after breakfast that morning, Thomas went to a mirror, brushed the hair back from his left forehead, and went to an upstairs bedroom where he shot himself in the left temple.

Could the screams heard by Lynne Thompson have been screams of the ghost of Ellen Wilkinson—like the screams that might have been heard when she went upstairs on that Christmas Eve morning to find her husband dead at his own hand?

Could the scent of perfume be one that Ellen wore? Could the bed have been moved by Thomas, so that the arrangement of the room was as he saw it for the last time?

Perhaps the ghost will only call on special occasions. It was in 1976, a hundred years after Thomas Wilkinson killed himself, that the

Thompsons moved in and started to restore the house he had built.

On June 19, 1992, when Mayor Gibbs and his family took over, they continued the restoration, added some new features in the yard, and made further plans. Will they meet any ghosts?

Why Does the Angel Cry?

Some unusual things have happened at the cemetery out at Parker's grove, along a graveled country road north and east of Shellsburg and not very far from town.

One of the unusual incidents happened the night Deanna and her friends went out to the cemetery. First they wandered around for a while, just sensing the somber mood of the burial grounds. The peaceful quiet impressed all of them. Then they noticed how varied the tombstones were in size and shape and age. They found that most of the older ones stood tall, and many of those were gray or white and dull and worn. Some of them had been reset on their bases. Others had broken corners or tops that had toppled off.

As dusk deepened into evening, someone noticed that those tall markers made shadows as varied as their shapes. On some of the very old ones, the lettering was so worn down that it was hardly visible; on others, lichens had grown to obliterate parts of the information. It was hard to trace the old ones to read the names and dates. As their fingers moved lightly over them, one of Deanna's friends said, "This must be a lot like how the blind read Braille."

Many of the more recent markers were either very tall or quite low. Some of the large ones marked a family plot, and smaller ones around them marked individual family members' graves. Some of those newer ones were more colorful and even sparkly. Names and dates on most of those were easy to read.

As she read some of the names out loud, one of the girls noticed that a few markers had birth dates from as early as 1865 and 1878, and she found one marked "b. 1885." But the death dates had not been recorded on those tombstones. When she mentioned that to the others, someone jokingly said, "They must be very old—too old, in fact, to still be living!"

Someone else said, "Gee, do you suppose they died but were never buried? Or maybe..."

Deanna interrupted that thought. She said, "I know what you were thinking. If they are still around, they'd have to be ghosts by now! Hey, you guys, we'd better be getting back to town. It's getting darkish and spooky out here and, besides, my tennies are soaked with dew."

Just then, Deanna came upon a marker shaped like an angel. That didn't scare her as much as the thought of ghosts roaming around among the tombstones or floating out from behind the next tall ones. While she was thinking about how pleasant and comforting it would be to have a friendly angel on a tombstone—maybe on her own some day—Deanna reached up and caressed the angel's face. It felt smooth, a little warm, and unexpectedly damp. She reached a little higher and rested her fingertips lightly and briefly just below the angel's eyes. Suddenly she jumped away and started running toward the car.

On the way to town, one of the others asked Deanna why she was in such a hurry to leave.

As soon as she caught her breath, Deanna answered, "Well, it was getting darker all the time, for being where we were. And we were talking about ghosts, too. But the scariest thing was when I reached up to the angel's eyes. They were wet."

"Oh, come on! Your hands must have been damp!"

"But they weren't. And I'm sure I felt tears coming from her eyes.

It wasn't dew, either. I had to lean on the angel to reach her face, and the rest of her was dry."

"Well, did that scare you?"

"Not just that. I'd been thinking about how comforting it could be to know an angel would be on my tombstone some day, to watch over me and keep me company. Then when I felt the tears, it struck me—it was more as if the angel wanted to be comforted."

Another girl said, "I've heard about that angel before, but I'd almost forgotten about it. Someone told me once that a lot of people have touched it, and the eyes and face felt wet, as if the angel was crying. That must be why they call her 'The Crying Angel.' Because of the tears. I think they say that grave is where a girl about our age was buried, long ago, but you can't read the stuff on the marker anymore."

But Deanna wonders if the crying angel marks the burial place of a girl her age who, for some reason unknown to others, was very unhappy when she died. And now that she has thought about it some more, she thinks the tears are a sign of the dead girl's lasting unhappiness. And since a monument can't cry, Deanna is a lot closer to believing in ghosts. Especially sad ghosts.

Wild Sweet Melodies

Beautiful branching elms used to line the carriage driveway that led up to the eighteen-room mansion. Built by an Irish immigrant named Keene and his wife, it was the scene of parties and teas. But that was all before the priest's curse.

Strong Irish Catholics, the Keenes came from their native country and made good in the new world. So good that they could buy large tracts of land close to a prospering northeast Iowa town, not far from the Mississippi River. They built a new home in the late 1800s, complete with servants' quarters.

A heavy donor to the local church, Keene had an argument with the priest. While no one is sure why it started or what it was about, there were witnesses to the end of the argument. Keene and the priest were arguing quite loudly and gesturing toward one another. In the end the priest, red with anger, raised his powerful voice and thundered down a curse on Keene. As Keene turned his back on the priest and stalked away, the priest also cursed his family and his grand new house.

Within a year, Keene died, leaving his wife and nine children. His wife died soon after, and six of the children left home. Although most were highly educated and did achieve financial success, tragedy befell them. At least one child was rumored to be insane, as evidenced by the thick iron bars covering the basement windows. The last descendant, a daughter, lived in the house for many years, teaching on the west coast in the winter and returning home for the summer. Over seventy-five years had passed since the home was built. The elms had grown old and were dying, their bark peeling off in strips to reveal smooth white wood. The trees creaked and swayed, tapping against the house and each other.

Neighbors reported that the daughter, an old lady by now, shut herself up in the house all day, playing the piano. They say sometimes the piano played itself, and late at night wild sweet melodies could be heard. A stranger stopped for a drink of water one day, unfamiliar with the town and the tales. He later reported that the water was red as blood and he was unable to drink a drop. Those who passed near the home reported a chill breeze in the hottest days of summer. Others said doors would be heard shutting constantly, even when the old lady was gone.

This last daughter died in the 1970s and the home was sold. The elms are gone and a new family lives there. But to this day they have never been able to get a babysitter to stay in the old house.

The Witch's Book

"You have had a hex put on you, cousin Ben. I am sure of it," said Rebecca.

"But why? And by whom? I have done no harm to anyone."

"No, but you have done well here. You are the richest farmer in Garber. Even those in Elkader and Guttenberg envy you."

"But how can you be so sure it is a hex?"

"You say the horse would not cross the old wooden bridge two days ago. The one not far from Plagman's barn, across Cedar Creek. At night, was it not?"

"Yes, Rebecca. It was cool and there were many shadows. I thought he was only afraid, although I have traveled that road with my buggy several times and he has never been afraid before." Ben shifted in his chair in the kitchen, scraping his rough boots on the wooden floor.

"And then?" Rebecca asked, leaning forward. Of medium height like Ben, she also had brown hair but very blue, intense eyes.

"And then today he would not cross it in the daylight. It was early this morning, very cool for August, and he shook and quivered like one possessed." Ben stopped speaking suddenly.

"Ben, I'm sure there is a hex on you!"

Ben shivered and leaned back in his chair, rubbing his pipe. "What must we do? I cannot live with a hex on me."

"I will talk to Henrietta Bitmorn. She has special powers."

Ben looked at her. "She is a witch then? She has a witch's book?"

"Do not say that! Do you want another hex? She is a good German like us but she has...special powers. She has a book. I will talk to her."

Rebecca walked the dusty road to Henrietta Bitmorn's house outside Garber. Few people visited her, except those with a special need, like Rebecca. A white-haired woman of indeterminate age, Henrietta was respected and somewhat feared. After listening closely to Rebecca's story, she agreed there was a hex on Ben. She would remove the hex that very night. Rebecca and Ben were to meet her at midnight at the bridge where the horse had balked.

Rebecca went with Ben in the buggy. No stars were out and the lanterns gave dim light. Ben's horse was more nervous than ever and whinnied and reared. They both tried to quiet the horse.

Suddenly, out of the dark night came a white apparition—straight toward them. Ben and Rebecca were even more frightened and they began muttering childhood prayers in their native tongue. The horse jerked back, trying to break free. As the apparition came closer, they realized it was human. It was Henrietta, dressed all in white with her white hair loose, seeming to float about her. When she was next to them, Ben and Rebecca could see she had a large black book in her hands, so black it could hardly be seen this night. Henrietta said nothing but held a hand to the horse's right eye and then to his left. The horse calmed and stood still.

Henrietta walked to the bridge and opened the black book. She began speaking in a language neither Ben nor Rebecca recognized and waving her arms in a strange pattern. Gradually, the sounds of the night disappeared. No crickets could be heard, no wind in the trees, no small creatures scurrying through the brush. Rebecca and Ben could no longer even hear the water tumbling under the bridge. They could see Henrietta's mouth move but heard nothing. She twisted slightly and looked at them. Somehow, they knew they must turn around and close their eyes.

They felt, not saw, a flash behind them. At first it was hot, so they were sweating, and then cold, so their teeth were chattering. Finally Henrietta laid the book down and lifted her arms. The night sounds returned and they could hear again. She asked them to face the bridge.

"The hex is gone now. You will not be bothered again," she said firmly. And then she was gone.

Ben prospered and was never troubled again. Upon his death, a large bequest was made to all living relatives of Henrietta Bitmorn.

Zelda Offers a Challenge

If you frequent the University of Northern Iowa campus and you're involved in any way with theater, you've probably met Zelda. Zelda is what the theater department people call the ghost that has been haunting Strayer-Wood Theater for over fifteen years.

Even when the theater department moved from the old auditorium building into Strayer-Wood in 1979, Zelda stayed with the department. She was practically considered a member by then. Many of the regulars were used to having her around.

At Strayer-Wood, when just one or two people are in the building at night, possibly closing up after a practice or later on, when a custodian is checking the lights and doors, those are the times when Zelda is likely to make her appearance.

In an article by Kelly Huggins in *The Northern Iowan* of May 4, 1990, Ms. Lorraine Commeret, an assistant professor of theater, was quoted as saying, "I'm positive there are spirits [in the theater]. Because of the intensity of the experience in theater, this would be a place to find spiritual activity." According to the same article, a theater major named Kristel Collett reported an experience. She told about how, just before she was to play her role during a performance of Shakespeare's *Twelfth Night*, someone from offstage came into the wing and said, 'Oh, excuse me,' and then turned to leave."

One can guess that it was a bit difficult for Kristel to execute her line perfectly after Zelda's appearance, but no one else noticed Zelda, so Kristel had to put up with a lot of teasing.

Lorraine says that Zelda appears in various parts of the theater. She herself had an encounter late one night when she was one of two persons who thought they were the only ones there. They were turning off lights in the south lobby. According to Huggins's article, Lorraine thought she saw someone sitting on a couch, but didn't know who or what it could be; she thought no one else was in the building.

The same Northern Iowan article told about others who by their experience have been led to believe that Zelda is a ghost that hangs around at the theater. Some claim they have heard screams "tearing through the theater" late at night. Others have witnessed a seeming accident that didn't hurt anyone because "someone" maneuvered the loose electrical cable and "unhooked [it so that] it fell into the only open seat in the house." As a result, some believe that Zelda is a protective ghost.

Zelda may have been a bit bewildered herself when she was hauled in a crate from the old building to Strayer-Wood. They say she has been relatively quiet for a few years now. So far, she has never harmed anyone. She may have startled some aspiring actors and actresses—maybe kept them on their toes or challenged them to do their best, or she would be ready to replace them.

About the Authors

Ruth D. Hein

Ruth D. Hein grew up in Van Horne, Iowa, as the middle child in a ghost-free Lutheran parsonage. With an M.A. from the University of Northern Iowa, she taught high school English and creative writing for 28 years, 21 of those in Decorah. Ruth now lives with her husband, Ken, on a small acreage near Worthington, Minnesota, where she collects ghost stories and wrote the historical column for the Worthington *Daily Globe* for 14 years.

Vicky L. Hinsenbrock

Vicky L. Hinsenbrock's German relatives loved to tell stories of the unexpected happenings when she was growing up in northeast Iowa. A graduate of Iowa State University with a major in animal science, she works for the USDA. She and her husband live in an old Victorian house in the country. No known ghosts inhabit their home.

Other books by Ruth D. Hein available through Adventure Publications:

Ghostly Tales of Minnesota

Other books by Ruth D. Hein:

More Ghostly Tales from Minnesota
Ghostly Tales of the Black Hills and Badlands
Eggplant Sandwiches (a collection of poems)
"...From the Face of the Earth..." (a pioneer story)

CP 7 13